A WORKBOOK ON
BIBLICAL STEWARDSHIP

A Workbook on
Biblical Stewardship

Richard E. Rusbuldt

WILLIAM B. EERDMANS PUBLISHING COMPANY
GRAND RAPIDS, MICHIGAN

Copyright © 1994 by Wm. B. Eerdmans Publishing Co.

255 Jefferson Ave. S.E., Grand Rapids, Michigan 49503

Printed in the United States of America

00 99 98 97 96 95 94   7 6 5 4 3 2 1

Library of Congress Cataloging-in-Publication Data

Rusbuldt, Richard E.
    A Workbook on biblical stewardship /
  Richard E. Rusbuldt.
      p.   cm.
    ISBN 0-8028-0723-2 (paper)
    1. Stewardship, Christian. 2. Christian giving. I. Title.
  BV772.R87   1994
  248′.6 — dc20   94-10493
                                            CIP

Contents

Preface

For many Christians, the phrase "time, talent, and tithe" has a familiar ring to it. Over the years, many of us have responded to the challenges of that phrase to be responsible in using our time, our God-given talents, and our money. The challenge continues.

More and more Christians appear to be willing to study and discuss what the Bible has to say about what God has entrusted to us. Christians who are serious about the Bible soon discover that God has said much about Christian stewards. And there is more to it than simply time, talent, and tithe. The material in this booklet has been written and tested in a variety of settings including seminars, seminaries, local churches, and an assortment of small groups. It is my sincere hope that many Christians will gain new insights from serious study and will accept new challenges in their journeys as stewards.

What follows would not exist without the assistance of a grand group of stewards who worked with me over a period of several years to refine my very unrefined grist! I say *thank you* to the following stewards: Donna Anderson, Dick Gladden, Louie Nelson, Alan Shumway, Karen Schwarz, Wendell Mettey, Jim Widmer, Bob Bouder, Edith Cober, Virginia Holmstrom, Ron Raught, Van Benschoten (deceased), Howard Washburn, Ray Weigum, and Debbie Haudkins.

One of the guidelines for writing this booklet was to keep the level of writing accessible to the broadest possible audience. A very special young steward, Ben Widmer, a seventh- and eighth-grade student during this period, helped immensely by telling me when I was at the wrong level! Special thanks also goes to Bob Roberts, executive director of World Mission Support for American Baptist Churches, USA, a very excellent model of a Christian steward, who worked with me to open doors to get the project completed.

Another special thanks goes to "chief steward" Ron Vallet, my longtime co-worker and friend, without whom this booklet probably would not have been published. He kept the vision going and opened numerous doors as well. In all the writing stages, my secretary was Lorie Custer, also a patient and caring steward, who saved both the project and my sanity at times!

I thank my editor, chief steward Tim Straayer, for the breath of life and vitality he has brought to these pages. All those who read and study these chapters will be blessed by his special gifts and keen insights.

Last, I thank the best steward of all — my dear wife, Flossie — who has read these chapters more times than any steward should have had to — and still says she loves me!

All of the above stewards are co-authors of this workbook.

Together, we offer it as a gift to you on *your* steward's journey.

1. What Is Biblical Stewardship?

Think of us in this way, as servants of Christ, and stewards of God's mysteries.

1 CORINTHIANS 4:1

A Brief Definition

Biblical stewardship is a way of living grounded in what the Bible tells us about our lives as God's people in God's created world. The Bible is God's guidebook for us as we seek to live as God's stewards. It contains stories of stewards from the past as well as guidance for us today. It is a book of hope and help that God has given us to let us know how we should care for all the things God has entrusted to us.

The Bible is a living book as well as a book about life. It is much more than a history text written in the past tense. It provides many references to God's hopes, plans, and promises to stewards, who are accounted "joint heirs" with Christ (Rom. 8:17) in God's family. Stewardship encompasses countless aspects of how we live our lives as Christians, and the Bible is our guidebook.

Who Is a Steward?

Every person who walks God's planet earth today is a steward. Some are good stewards — caring, careful, attentive, compassionate, thoughtful, committed, and generous. And unfortunately some are poor stewards — careless, wasteful, thoughtless, inconsiderate, self-centered, and hurtful.

My little granddaughter and I walked along a country road near our home picking wild clover for a bouquet for her grandmother. With hands almost full, she spotted a discarded soda can. "Look," she said, "let's take that with us for recycling," and she ran to pick it up. Not much later we saw an empty beer can sail out the window of a passing car. As my granddaughter ran to pick that one up, too, it occurred to me that examples of good and bad stewardship are just that common and close at hand every day.

A friend of mine does his own oil changes. For a long time, he used to dump the dirty oil behind his garage when the job was done. Now he's more sensitive to the issue, and he takes care to bring the used oil to a recycling center. But years after he stopped discarding the oil, the dirt behind his garage is still dirty and grimy, and nothing grows there. Our stewardship decisions can have long-lasting consequences. I've learned some lessons in stewardship over the years, too. There was a time when I used to let the water run while I brushed my teeth. Two or three times a day, a lot of water would go uselessly down the drain. Now I make the effort to preserve a precious resource by turning on the faucet only when I really need the water. It's a small thing, but it's important — and so is the attitude that motivates the action.

The Bible describes many stewards. Eve and Adam were the first. God placed in their care all that had been created (Gen. 1:28-30) — quite a responsibility! Then there was Noah, into whose care God entrusted all the species of life at a time when the world was to be destroyed through a flood (Gen. 7:1-4). Jesus and his disciples were good stewards when the crowd that had followed them into a desert place stayed long enough to become hungry. They found food (five loaves of bread and two fish), and with Jesus' blessing it proved to be enough for everyone to eat. In fact, the disciples gathered twelve basketfuls of leftovers and continued to be good stewards of God's bountiful blessings (Matt. 14:13-21).

Of course, not all the stewards mentioned in the Bible were good and faithful in their exercise of stewardship. Ananias and Sapphira lost their lives when they lied about their role as stewards of what God had entrusted to them (Acts 5:1-11).

Stewards of God's Mysteries

In 1 Corinthians 4:1, Paul says that Christians are "servants of Christ and stewards of God's mysteries." The first readers of Paul's letter readily understood the sort of relationship Paul was saying should exist between them and God's mysteries. Today, however, the word *steward* isn't used all that much in everyday conversation. We most typically think of stewards as the employees on boats and planes who serve food and see to the comfort of the passengers. In Paul's day, however, a steward was a servant (usually a slave) who was entrusted with the authority to manage all of a master's household affairs. It was a position of considerable trust and responsibility. In this passage, then, Paul is saying that Christians are humble servants of Christ but that they have been specially chosen and elevated to the position of managing God's household. They have been selected to undertake the responsibility of caring for God's mysteries. What are God's mysteries?

The universe is full of mysteries. The more scientists discover, the more mysteries they seem to unfold. Astronomers recently detected an incredibly bright light coming from a source that is estimated to be at least fifty million light-years away. A light-year is the distance that light, traveling at roughly 186,000 miles per second, covers in a year — just shy of 6 trillion miles. So 50 million light-years is about 300 million trillion miles, a distance so great as to defy human comprehension. No one can say for certain what it is that is shining so brightly out there. It's a mystery. Still, there is hope that with further investigation, astronomers will be able to unravel this puzzle as they have so many others.

There is another class of mysteries that remain beyond hope of explanation during our lives here on earth. For example, who can explain the transformation that takes place in a damaged, hurting, sinful life when it is touched by the transforming power of Christ? Christians rejoice when such conversions take place, but who among us can explain them? Scripture likens the working of the Spirit to the wind, which "blows where it chooses" (John 3:8). This is one of the mysteries of God that Paul refers to. We cannot hope to explain it, but that is not to say that it is not a worthwhile effort to try to understand what we can.

It is part of our obligation as Christian stewards to probe the mysteries of our covenant with God. The effort provides not only excitement, mystery, and intrigue but also a great amount of satisfaction when learning takes place. May your new insights be many as you probe the meanings of biblical stewardship in this nine-chapter journey.

The Bible and Stewardship

The stewardship story begins in Genesis 1 and is woven through all of biblical and human history. God took the initiative through an act of self-revelation in the pages of the Bible to communicate to us the meaning of life — past, present, and future.

God's word, as it is found in the Bible, came together over the centuries. The Bible is not always easy to understand, nor is it ever completely understood. However, it can stimulate both faith and practice, since it presents God's point of view on many issues. For instance, there are suggestions in the Bible about what God would like to have happen in our lives. For those who search, the Bible has much to say about who God is, what God wants, how we can be partners, and what we should do with what God has entrusted to us.

Biblical stewardship flows from God's side of the relationship between the Creator and the created world. The Bible tells the story of a partnership between God and Christian stewards working together for the good of all creation. In our study of biblical stewardship, we will search for statements, suggestions, and guidelines that have been revealed to God's people over the centuries.

As you begin this study, you will do well to keep these key points in mind:

1. The Bible informs us about God's points of view on the meanings and purposes of life.
2. The Bible gives us information about God's hopes and plans for all creation.
3. The Bible emphasizes that God is a God of hope.
4. From beginning to end, the Bible stresses the interrelationship of all aspects of creation.
5. The Bible gives us information about the role of the Christian steward as a partner in God's plans.

Your study of biblical stewardship will help you understand what it means to be a steward of God's mysteries. Through Christ we become joint heirs of God the Father — that is to say, full members of God's family (Rom. 8:17). We don't just "work" for God. Part of the wonderful mystery is that we are brought into God's household and entrusted with God's priceless mysteries.

Biblical Stewardship and Links with Life

Think about your current ideas regarding biblical stewardship. Circle each term in the following list that you feel has some connection with it.

possessions	money	tithing
ownership	laws	power
freedom	soil	church collections
home	managing something	salaries
riches	rules	environment
poverty	sharing	responsibility
employment	buying things	recycling
God's rules	taking care of	love
the world	something for	joy
gifts	someone else	disposable income
time	tax breaks	grace
justice	the poor	

The first stewardship link we make is usually with money. Even when they think specifically of *biblical* stewardship, most people still think of money. After all, money is important. Jesus spoke more about money and possessions than about any other subject. In our culture, we tend to be very sensitive about everything connected with money. We are suspicious of people we think might be trying to get us to part with some of it. After all, it's "our" money. We tend to be secretive about how much we earn, how much we save, how much we give away. In general, we are highly protective of what we possess — sometimes to the point of acting as though we feel that even God had better not touch it!

A lot of people complain that all the church wants is money. They single out the church for this sort of criticism even though they don't take special note of the fact that banks, gasoline stations, insurance companies, grocery stores, movie theaters, golf courses — and just about everybody else you could name — is seeking their money seven days a week. Somehow it's different if their church asks for money out of a sincere desire to do God's will and be God's people.

Our Culture and Ownership Society

We should always try to understand what the Bible has to say about stewardship by looking at its implications within the context of our own lives. What is the meaning of biblical stewardship in North America? We live in an "ownership" society. We "own" houses, cars, bicycles, televisions, CD's, stocks and bonds, stereo systems, real estate, and many other things. And if we don't own them, we are told that we ought to own them! Voices shout from newspapers, television, radio, magazines, and billboards that the meaning of life is all tied up with wanting more and getting more. Rarely does anyone talk about giving more or sharing more. Seldom do we hear about Jesus' suggestion to the young man who inquired about the meaning of life: "Sell your possessions, and give the money to the poor . . . ; then come, follow me" (Matt. 19:21).

Why are we so obsessed with acquiring possessions, with ownership? How can Christians — people who are "bought with a price" — escape the cultural quicksand of always wanting more things? How do Christians reconcile biblical teachings about possessions with their desire to own and acquire more? Consider the implications of 1 Chronicles 29:11, 14, 16: "Yours, O LORD, are the greatness, the power, the glory, the victory, and the majesty; for all that is in the heavens and on the earth is yours; yours is the kingdom, O LORD, and you are exalted as head above all. . . . But who am I, and what is my people, that we should be able thus to make this freewill offering? *For all things come from you, and of your own have we given you.* . . . O LORD, our God, all this abundance that we have provided for building you a house for your holy name comes *from your hand and is all your own.*" In Psalm 24:1, the writer says, "The earth is the LORD's and all that is in it." That's pretty clear. According to Paul, we don't even "own" ourselves (1 Cor. 6:19)!

For some additional biblical thoughts on the concept of ownership, see the following passages: Psalm 50:10-11; 89:11-12; Leviticus 25:23; Ezekiel 18:4; Haggai 2:8; 1 Corinthians 6:19; Matthew 6:33; Acts 16:17; Romans 14:8.

Some History of Ownership

Legend has it that the city of Rome was founded by two brothers, Romulus and Remus, and that in the early days of the city, Romulus distributed a *heredium* (about one acre of land) to every citizen, conferring on them the "right of ownership" to the land. Roman law emerged in this context, grounded in an "absolute conception of ownership." According to Charles Avila in his book *Ownership: Early Christian Teaching,* this understanding of ownership involves "the unrestricted right of control over a physical thing, and whosoever has this right can claim the thing he owns wherever it is, no matter who possesses it." The Romans even extended the concept of ownership to include not only things but people: slaves were assets — economic "things." It was this kind of culture into which Jesus Christ was born.

And, to a very substantial extent, this is the kind of culture into which we have been born as well. The obsession to own more, get more, and have more dominates our society. The world of advertising is built on this foundation, as is much of our economic way of life. Children seem to come into life with a tendency to view things in terms of what belongs to them and what doesn't. How quickly a child grasps a toy or a piece of candy and shouts "Mine!" Many children are taught from their earliest days that it is all right to want and get more rather than to share.

And the hunger for more seems to be growing. In a survey released as we moved into the 1990s, Jacqueline Silver, executive vice president and director of research for Backer Spielvogel Bates Worldwide, Inc., said, "Materialism will continue to be one of the driving forces in American society over the next decade, and an increasingly important force in other major [world] markets as well. In a clear break with traditional values, consumers are no longer ashamed to admit that their primary goals are to own expensive things and lead luxurious lifestyles." How can today's Christians live within an ownership culture and not be transformed by it?

Two Stewardship Models

What does all this thinking about owning things have to do with biblical stewardship? Everything. There are two basic models to consider when analyzing North American life today. One is the ownership model to which most North Americans are introduced at birth. The other is the biblical stewardship model. When you become a Christian, you have the opportunity to learn about and practice the biblical model. Paul said that at first Christians are "babes in Christ" but that we grow in our understanding of God's will for our lives and our partnership with God. This growth inevitably involves growth in stewardship.

God's model for the way we should be related to other people and the larger created world is found in the Bible. From Genesis to Revelation we can read of the unfolding of God's relationships and expectations for all creation. Christian stewardship involves the faithful, wise, and responsible management of all that God has entrusted to us — for God's purposes, not our own. Christian stewardship takes in all of God's created order — time, physical resources, the planet we call home, human life itself, our spiritual gifts, relationships with other people, and the Good News of our salvation in Christ.

From earliest history, human beings have sought and developed rules and laws. The Bible's stories of beginnings suggest that God had some rules for humans to live with, too. Compare the emphases of the two models described below.

Ownership Model	Biblical Stewardship Model
Human rules	God's rules
Human ownership	God's ownership
Society's laws carry the threat of punishment, even death	God's grace promises salvation through Christ, forgiveness
Stratified community: the rich rule by power	Covenant community: joint heirs, one household
"It is mine"	"It is God's"
rarely entrusted	entrusted to stewards
receive	return
keep	share
take	give
now	forever
me	you
I	we

These models define two different perspectives and, indeed, two different sorts of worlds. Give some thought to which model governs your outlook and behavior most of the time. Are you satisfied that you have developed a biblically appropriate view of the world? Can you think of specific areas in which you'd like to shift from the ownership model to the biblical stewardship model?

The Seed of Stewardship Grows

When you became a Christian, you made an outright decision to do so. You chose Christ, perhaps over a number of other options. It takes an act of the heart, mind, and body to become a Christian (Rom. 10:9-10). Nor do Christians casually decide to become stewards. You become a steward when you become a Christian. Once you belong to Christ, the steward seed is there; it grows as it is tended. How you handle what God entrusts to you is the heart of stewardship. You start the stewardship journey as a beginner, a learner.

To journey as a Christian steward is to learn how to grow in caring for and responding to all that God has entrusted to you. As it was in the days of Joshua, so it is today. Joshua said, "Now if you are unwilling to serve the LORD, choose this day whom you will serve, whether the gods your fathers served in the region beyond the River or the gods of the Amorites in whose land you are living; but as for me and my household, we will serve the LORD" (Josh. 24:15). Or as we might put it today, "If you are having problems with your current lifestyle, choose this day which lifestyle you will lead, whether it will be the North American 'get and get more' model or the biblical model."

The Christian lifestyle is a matter of faithful response to God rather than accommodation to the culture. If God's Spirit is not vital within us, there is no way to avoid being absorbed fully into our culture. It takes prayer, courage, wisdom, strength, Bible study, and support from other Christians to see and understand the biblical model. It takes the same ingredients to put it into practice (Matt. 7:13-14). Needless to say, growing as a steward is best done with other Christians.

Choose Your Stewardship Model

It appears that most Christians today are looking for middle ground between the two lifestyle models. We lean more naturally to the cultural than to the stewardship model. We *are* a part of our culture. It wasn't much different in Jesus' time. The young ruler wanted to know how to gain eternal life. Since he professed that he was already keeping the commandments, Jesus then told him to take the next step, to sell what he owned, give to the poor, and follow him. The young man went away sorrowing, for he was rich (Matt. 19:20-22). Some searchers today have a similar reaction. What persuades you more when making decisions — the Bible or the culture?

Can God and wealth be served at the same time? Jesus said no (Matt. 6:24). This makes it a difficult subject for Christians to discuss. It's not easy to turn our backs on devotion to either God or wealth. But the Bible, in both the Old and New Testaments, is clear: if we are God's people, we are expected to be and to live differently. For example, we will not waste the world and its resources — we will preserve them and care for them. God does not command us to abandon the system within which we live. To the contrary, God calls us to be accountable for it, responsible for it, each in our own way. God calls all of us to abandon devotion to money, but God does not tell all of us that we have to stay out of banks. God calls all of us to abandon devotion to the world, but God does not tell all of us that we have to withdraw to a cloister or monastery. God wants us to be in the world, influencing both individual lives and human systems as the Bible teaches us to, providing a benefit to our sisters and brothers — and to ourselves in the process. We are to be like Christ, whose garment was seamless, who came eating and drinking, and yet who gave everything — even his life. Granted, his was a tough act to follow, but it is a goal toward which we must strive. You and I can't choose both worlds. We have to choose each day which model we will use as our guide in living our life for Christ.

As you think about stewardship, keep in mind both the role of the individual and the role of the church. Few congregations think of themselves as a body of stewards beyond the matter of paying the church budget. For many years stewardship has been too narrowly defined as a "money for the church" issue. There has been a tendency to forget that all decisions about witness, ministry, and service emerge from biblical stewardship.

Take another look at the list on page 5. If you left any of the items uncircled, can you explain your reasons for doing so? Are there areas of life over which we are not called to exercise stewardship, things we are not competent to care for? Now think a while about your own life journey. How do the Bible's teachings on stewardship influence your life? For instance, the act of regularly supporting your church financially has a biblical base. So does supporting mission beyond your church, giving a portion of your time to Christ's work in your church or community, and many other Christian actions. Make a list of the ways your daily life is affected by the stewardship model. How are you managing? What are you sharing? How are you growing in your stewardship?

1. _____

_____

2. _____

_____

3. _____

_____

4. _____

_____

5. _____

_____

6. _____

_____

7. _____

_____

8. _____

_____

9. _____

_____

10. _____

_____

Next, list some stewardship issues that may be problems or even mysteries for you. Identify things you don't understand how to handle, things you are ignoring or avoiding, or perhaps biblical concepts with which you disagree.

1. _____

_____

2. _____

_____

3. _____

_____

4. _____

_____

Finally, list ways in which you believe your church is modeling good stewardship in Christ's name.

1. _____

_____

2. _____

_____

3. _____

_____

4. _____

_____

5. _____

_____

6. _____

_____

In the pages that follow, you will be challenged to consider different aspects of biblical stewardship, though we'll scarcely be exhausting the subject. The Bible addresses almost everything a steward does about all of life. Read on, and share the steward's journey. Breathe a prayer that God's Spirit will help you clear away cultural cobwebs and shine a new light so you can see new truths as a growing Christian.

QUESTIONS FOR DISCUSSION:

1. What are your reactions to the subject of biblical stewardship?

2. What tensions are there in your own life between the ownership model and the biblical stewardship models?

3. Do you feel it is possible to live as part of an ownership society while being a true follower of Jesus Christ? How?

4. In what ways are the life and ministry of your congregation built on a biblical stewardship model? On an ownership model?

5. When was the last time you talked about biblical stewardship with somebody else? Participated in a Sunday school lesson on biblical stewardship? Listened to a sermon on biblical stewardship? If your

church is not adequately focused on the responsibilities of Christian stewardship, what can you do to change that situation? Would you be willing to do it?

6. How do you feel when your pastor preaches on the subject of money, and what you do with it?

7. Do you have a stewardship problem or mystery you would like to share with your group?

2. Stewardship Is Entrusting

*I am not ashamed, for I know the one in whom I
have put my trust, and I am sure that he is able to
guard until that day what I have entrusted to him.*

2 TIMOTHY 1:12

When was the last time you handed something to someone else to take
care of for you? I can remember once when my four-year-old granddaughter Kenya was getting ready to leave our house after a visit and she
handed her favorite doll, Angel, to me. "I want you to take care of her for
me," she said. As I held the doll, I couldn't help but smile, but to her it was
no laughing matter. She told me she would want her doll back the same
way she had given her to me. As I looked at Angel's badly bruised right eye,
her disheveled clothing, and lack of shoes and socks, it occurred to me that
I might be able to do better than that. When Kenya entrusted Angel to me,
I became a steward of the doll, commissioned to care for her on Kenya's
behalf.

Perhaps you've experienced handing over something precious of your
own to someone else for safekeeping — a house, a pet, or even a child. Most
parents are anxious the first time they leave a child with a baby-sitter, even if
the sitter is a grandparent or a close friend. How did you feel the last time
you handed over something important to someone else? How did it work out?
Was your trust well placed?

14

Most of what is written about Christian stewardship today stresses *managing* — and quite rightly so. But a couple of other essential ingredients are frequently overlooked or at least shortchanged in such discussion: *entrusting* and *confronting*. I'd like to spend some time looking more closely at each of these elements. We'll take up the issue of entrusting in this chapter, the issue of care-managing in Chapter 3, and the issue of confronting in Chapter 4.

You Have to Let Go

Before I can manage something for you, you must first entrust it to me. The more valuable a thing is to you, the harder it will be to turn it over to anyone else. Most parents will experience some uneasiness — if not outright fear — entrusting the family car to a sixteen-year-old with a brand new driver's license. Most sixteen-year-olds give their parents some reason to question their common sense from time to time. If the family has only one car, it can be a real test of trust to turn over the keys. But trust is the lifeblood of a healthy relationship, and it's essential to personal growth within that relationship.

We cannot learn to become good stewards unless someone is willing to trust us first. Parents have a special opportunity to help their children get experience at being stewards within the arena of their love and care. But however tentative and protective the parents may try to be in such efforts, the process will necessarily involve their letting go of something that is valuable to them and trusting their children to care for it responsibly.

It's never easy to let go of something that you treasure. There is always the possibility that your trust will not be honored, and that can lead to disappointment, hurt, and even serious trouble. But when someone honors your trust by doing an excellent job, you both can feel good about it, and each of you will have grown in your relationship together.

Biblical Records of Entrusting

The Bible offers significant illustrations of entrusting. God spoke out of a burning bush, and turned the future of the people of Israel over to Moses (Exod. 3:1-12). Moses asked, "Who am I that I should go to Pharaoh, and bring the Israelites out of Egypt?" and God replied, "I will be with you. . . . It is I who sent you." God was saying, "I am turning over to you, Moses, the future of my people. Now, get going!"

In the Gospels we read that while Jesus hung on the cross, he entrusted the care of his mother to John (John 19:26-27). In Acts 1:8 we read that Jesus launched a worldwide partnership by entrusting much of the future of his ministry to those who would be his "witnesses in Jerusalem, in all Judea and Samaria, and to the ends of the earth." As Christian stewards, we are engaged in a partnership in mission with God and one another, under the leadership of the Holy Spirit. Jesus' expression of trust has been passed on through each generation of disciples to us today.

In many of his parables, Jesus places the act of entrusting at the heart of the story. In the parable of the talents (Matt. 25:14-30), the one going on a journey called the servants together and "entrusted his property to them." The Samaritan turned over the care of the man who had been beaten and robbed to the innkeeper (Luke 10:29-39). The Samaritan served as a steward, and then, through his entrusting, he made the innkeeper a steward as well. Jesus' story of the prodigal son (Luke 15:11-32) gives us many different views of stewardship and trust both honored and dishonored in the relationships between the father and his two sons and the ways in which each dealt with the father's estate and his share of the inheritance.

In 1 Timothy 4:10, Paul told a youthful Timothy that it was no small thing to be entrusted with the gospel. Sharing the Good News was going to involve "toil and struggle." But the rewards would make the effort worthwhile. In 2 Timothy 2:2, Paul told him, "What you have heard from me through many witnesses entrust to faithful people who will be able to teach others as well." At that time in history, God entrusted to Paul and a few others the spread of the gospel in the Mediterranean world. It was a major task for a small group of stewards, but they accepted the trust and gave thanks to God for entrusting the gospel to them.

Entrusting in Daily Life

We are constantly entrusting things to others and in turn being entrusted to care for things of theirs in everyday life. We take these transactions of trust for granted, even though they often involve our health and wealth, even our spiritual welfare.

Every time we deposit money in a bank, we trust the banker (and the government, which insures the deposit) to protect, invest it wisely, and provide a reasonable rate of interest. Every time we eat in a restaurant, we trust staff to prepare and serve us food that is safe. Every time we climb into a taxi or board a bus or book passage on a ship or an airplane, we trust that we will be taken safely to our destination. Every time we take our own cars in for service or repairs, we trust that the mechanic will return them to us in a safe operating condition. Every time we check into a hospital, we trust that the doctors and staff are well trained and competent and have our best interests in mind. Every time we drop our children off at school or a day-care facility, we trust that they will be protected from harm and taught properly.

Of course, our trust is not always repaid. Banks go bust. People get food poisoning at restaurants. Airplanes crash. Mechanics rip people off. Doctors engage in malpractice. Children get shot in school. But these thankfully rare exceptions can serve to make us more thankful for the good stewardship we receive most of the time and encourage us to be better stewards ourselves. We appreciate and value good stewards. So does God.

The Entrusting God

We find references to entrusting in the very first pages of the Bible, in the creation accounts in Genesis 1 and 2. English translations of these accounts obscure the fact that two different Hebrew words are used for God. Genesis 1 uses the word *Elohim,* which means "the one supreme deity," and hence underscores the cosmic extent of the relationship of the one supreme God to the whole of the creation. Genesis 2 uses the Hebrew word *Yahweh,* which is often translated "the LORD." It is a proper noun, a personal name of the divine, and as such it underscores the personal aspect of God's relationships with human beings. In the Old Testament, God spoke to the patriarchs as friends.

It is first under the name *Elohim* that the Scriptures describe God as entrusting. Read Genesis 1:26-31. There God says, "Let humankind be good stewards over the fish of the sea and of the sea itself, over the birds of the air and the air itself, and over the cattle of the field and the soil itself, over all the earth itself, and over every creeping thing that creeps on and inside the earth" (my translation). At the outset, God turned over to humans everything that had been created. God was willing to trust the first two persons and their offspring to manage capably what had been so carefully created. When the days of creating were complete, God observed that the creation was good. We can assume everything was in good shape when the earth and heavens were turned over to us.

Notice that at no point do we read that God gave us title to anything — not even a plot of ground. God entrusts humans with what can be an enjoyable task but retains overall ownership and a will for creation. As stewards, we seek to know God's will and then to do it.

Now look at the second chapter of Genesis, which provides a different version of the same story. Here we find God portrayed as a Personal Friend. As it was then, so it is today: the supreme Creator is a personal friend to us as well and speaks to us as persons. Take time to consider this question: What is God, your Friend, saying to you about stewardship today?

At no point does the Bible indicate that God left the scene after entrusting the care of everything to men and women. The entire Bible gives one message: "God and we are in this together." Our personal Friend has not left us alone in the midst of creation. "We can say with confidence, 'The Lord is my helper; I will not be afraid,'" because God has promised, "I will never leave you or forsake you" (Heb. 13:5-6). Jesus said, "Where two or three are gathered in my name, I am there among them" (Matt. 18:20), and he promised to be with us always (Matt. 28:20). As God's stewards, we can be certain that we do not stand or serve alone.

It is important to note that one steward can make a significant difference. One reason for this is that God is in partnership with each steward. Guidance, support, and courage are available in plentiful supply from our Partner.

In Genesis 3 the story moves on to describe how humans quickly violated God's trust, how they introduced sin, guilt, and suffering into the good creation. The rest of the Old Testament is an account of how God worked to build a new relationship with humans. God cared. God acted to lead and guide. The people of God made efforts to follow, but after a time they always abandoned those efforts and lapsed into rejecting and cursing their Creator and Friend. Through it all, God continued to promise his care for them. God yearned for a renewed relationship with Israel throughout the whole of the the Old Testament period, during the generations of the judges, the kingdom, and the prophets.

Despite the long history of Israel's rejection, in the fullness of time, the steadfast God sent his Son Jesus Christ to redeem the lost. This was the pinnacle of God's efforts to reach out and create a living, loving relationship with "all who have sinned." The cost to God was inconceivable, unmatched by any human sacrifice in history, but it was gloriously rewarded. Beyond the ugly cross and the sealed tomb, God provided resurrection. That is the measure of how much God wanted — and continues to want — to relate to us.

God Entrusted Us with the Good News

God meets us in relationships. God entrusted the Good News of a new relationship to us before anything else, and that is truly good news! The seeking, caring, loving God described in Genesis 3 is the same God who searches for us, cares for us, and loves us today. We read in 1 John 4:9-10 that "God's love was revealed among us in this way: God sent his only Son into the world so that we might live through him. In this is love, not that we loved God, *but that he loved us and sent his Son to be the atoning sacrifice for our sins.*"

Part of the Good News that God has entrusted to us is God's desire that "all might believe." It is God's will that we should live free from hurt, wrongs, and oppression. God aches for those who are hooked on drugs and those who sleep in cardboard boxes and huddle on heating grates because they have no homes. God is wounded when children are abused and molested in their own homes, when older people are beaten and abused, cheated and put down. God cares for every person on the face of the earth. And God's greatest gift, the Good News, cries out to the world that God cares. God entrusted this great news to Christian stewards.

Those of us who get caught up in the busyness of running churches, of preparing new programs and paying the bills for new construction, upkeep, and services, can easily make a tragic mistake: if we don't take care to review our priorities, we can end up spending more time with checkbooks and calendars than we do with the Bible, the steward's guidebook. Today's stewards need to keep searching out God's messages to us in the Bible.

Some Christians also make the tragic mistake of thinking only of money whenever the word *stewardship* is mentioned, as if money were the only thing that God had entrusted to us. The first and most important thing God has entrusted to us is the Good News, God's promises that "I love you," "I died for you," and "I will give you a new beginning." God is very much concerned with what you and I are doing with the Good News. The ways in which we manage our money and possessions to proclaim and/or implement the Good News in a needy, hurting world is also a Godly concern, but it is secondary, derivative. Whatever the day of final accounting turns out to be for Christians, it's not likely that God's first question to us will be "What did you do with your money?" but "What did you do with the Good News I entrusted to you?"

I heard a beautiful story about stewards and God's Good News involving an elderly Christian woman in Russia. One evening, a visitor to her church observed her talking with her pastor after the service and noted that she was crying and visibly distressed. The visitor approached the pastor later to ask whether something serious had happened to the woman. The pastor explained that in January of that year, the woman made a commitment to God to be instrumental in bringing one person to Christ each month. But her failing health had limited her activity, and now as the year was drawing to a close, she wept to report that she had managed to win only seven people to God!

There are stewards who take very seriously their commission to proclaim the Good News God has entrusted to them.

Celebrate What God Has Entrusted to You

Christians need not be fearful of what God has entrusted to us or the responsibilities implied by that trust. Instead, we should celebrate the fact that God thinks highly enough of us to be willing to turn over the Good News and so many other things to us. Take a couple of minutes to list some of the things that you are especially grateful to God for having entrusted to you:

_____

_____

_____

_____

_____

_____

_____

_____

Now list some ways in which you are being a steward of God's Good News:

_____

_____

_____

_____

_____

_____

_____

_____

_____

Entrusting Is a Two-Way Street

Let's face it: contemplating the challenges and difficulties of managing God's Good News can be overwhelming. It encompasses our lives, our spiritual gifts, and all our relationships, time, money, possessions, resources — and everything else God has created. Just thinking about it can make a person tired.

At times it may seem almost unfair that God has put the responsibility for all this wealth of people, relationships, and things on our shoulders. But God doesn't just unload this burden on us and then walk away. To begin with, we are stewards together: God works with each of us to enable, support, encourage, and supply resources, strength, and vision — whatever we need to be stewards. Second, God takes up the role of steward, too, safeguarding the valuable things that we entrust to divine care. As Paul put it, "I know the one in whom I have put my trust, and I am sure that he is able to guard until that day what I have entrusted to him" (2 Tim. 1:12). This last phrase can be translated in several ways. In the Good News Bible, the text reads, "what he has entrusted to me," but a note cites as an alternate reading, "what I have entrusted to him." Similar alternative readings are cited in notes in other translations. The Phillips paraphrase reads, "the work [God] has committed to me is safe in [God's] hands."

We Christians have committed ourselves — our souls — to God. As Christians, we can be secure in the belief that God takes care of us on our earthly journey. God is fully capable of guaranteeing our souls eternal fellowship with God. God is the steward of your soul, a good steward you can count on for eternity. God has entrusted many things to us, and we can entrust many things to God. Entrusting is truly a two-way street.

You have already listed some things God has entrusted to you. Now make a list of some things you have entrusted to God. For example, most Christians find confidence in the belief that God has prepared a life beyond death for them; they have entrusted their future to God. Trusting implies a continuing relationship, with active participation in the trust by both parties.

_____

_____

_____

_____

_____

_____

_____

_____

Are there things in your life that you should entrust to God and haven't yet? Things you have specifically resisted turning over to God? Make a list of these:

_____

_____

_____

_____

_____

_____

_____

_____

By way of conclusion, let's take another look at the points we have raised in this chapter:

1. Before we can manage anything, it must first be entrusted, turned over to us.
2. God has entrusted much to us — most importantly God's Good News, but also such concerns as life, relationships, our earthly environment, money, possessions, time, and spiritual gifts.
3. We, in turn, are encouraged to entrust things — including the well-being of our souls — to God.

QUESTIONS FOR DISCUSSION

1. Share an experience in which you entrusted something of value to someone else and were either gratified or disappointed in the result. How specifically did this experience affect your willingness to trust someone else with something important? Can you name any specific ways in which it affected your willingness to trust God?

2. Name some ways in which Christians serve as stewards of the Good News of Jesus Christ that God has entrusted to us. Are there any specific ways in which every Christian has a responsibility to respond to that trust? For example, do you believe that every Christian has a responsibility to offer a personal witness to strangers?

3. In what ways are you and God partners in your journey? During the past year, what aspect of this partnership has given you the most trouble? The most joy?

4. In what area do you think your church has most effectively responded to the trust that God has placed in it? In what area do you think it has fallen the farthest short? Name one thing your church could do to improve this shortcoming most effectively.

5. What sort of witness do you think it is most important for Christians to make concerning their loving, caring, redeeming God? Can you point to ways in which you are making this sort of witness in your own life? In the life of your church?

3. Stewardship Is Care-Managing

Therefore be imitators of God, as beloved children,
and live in love, as Christ loved us and gave himself
up for us, a fragrant offering and sacrifice to God.

EPHESIANS 5:1-2

In the previous chapter I mentioned the occasion on which my granddaughter Kenya turned her rather beat-up doll, Angel, over to me for safekeeping. When I accepted her trust, I became a "manager" of Angel's well-being on behalf of Kenya. What did that entail? What was I supposed to do? How are Christian stewards supposed to respond when God entrusts us with so much of value? The Bible tells us about the sort of response that God is looking for.

The Biblical Meaning of the Word Steward

The Bible uses several words for *steward*. In general, they all refer to someone who is put in charge of something for someone else. The Old Testament contains four such Hebrew words which indicate that a steward is someone "over a house," "one who is over (something)," the "head of" something, or the "chief." In the New Testament, the word most frequently used in this

24

regard is *oikonomos,* which means "one who has the responsibility for the planning and administering (*nomos* = to put in order) the affairs of a household (*oikos*) that belongs to someone else." These stewards, sometimes called servants, were responsible for much more than money. They were obliged to provide hospitality, kindness, services, and food. Beyond these things, they were to see to the protection and maintenance of the householder's buildings, animals, trees, environment, institutions, time, schedules, skills, clothing, and general welfare.

Scholars tell us that the Hebrew and Greek words for *steward* came into old English through the word *stigweard* — *stig* meaning part or all of a house, and *weard* meaning "warden" or "keeper." Hence, a steward was a housekeeper, a "keeper of a room or house for someone else."

Jesus Adds a New Meaning

Jesus provided a number of illustrations about what it means to be a good steward. One of the best known is found in John 10, where Jesus talks about the good shepherd. In Jesus' day, shepherds were hired to take care of flocks of sheep, often numbering in the hundreds. It was a lonely job in the hills away from the villages. There were many dangers, such as wild animals, for both sheep and shepherd. It was the shepherd's task to care for the sheep and keep them from danger.

In verses 12 and 13 we read that Jesus said, "The hired hand, who is not the shepherd and does not own the sheep, sees the wolf coming and leaves the sheep and runs away — and the wolf snatches them and scatters them. The hired hand runs away because a hired hand does not care for the sheep." Even if you don't know anything about shepherds and sheep, the message is quite clear: Jesus injected the notion of *care* as a critical part of being a steward.

Present Meaning of the Word Manager

Today many people think of a steward as a kind of manager. The term *manager* typically makes us think of the business world. Most managers we know take care of stores, banks, garages, theaters, and the like. They either manage something directly or manage a staff of people who do. As a rule, people who work under supervision tend to have strong feelings about their managers, ranging from strong respect and loyalty to scorn and contempt. Most of those feelings are predictable responses to management styles.

Managers who are able to show that they genuinely care about their employees earn their devotion far more often than managers who are interested only in the bottom line.

How people manage their own jobs often provides clues to how much they care about them. The more people care about what it is they're doing, the greater the effort they will put into doing their best. People who hate their jobs may do them well in spite of their feelings, but their attitude will usually be evident in some way. Reflect on the job you hold now (as an employee, homemaker, or the like) or a job you held in the past and check any of the statements in the following list that apply in connection with it.

_____ I like my work.

_____ I hate my work.

_____ I take pride in my work.

_____ I make enough money to support my household, but I'm not very interested in what I'm doing.

_____ I get a real sense of fulfillment from my job.

_____ I'd do better work if I thought it was appreciated.

_____ I consider the people I work with to be my friends.

_____ I don't really feel much connection with other people where I work.

_____ I managed to get the job I wanted.

_____ I wound up with the job I've got largely because of other people's expectations of me.

_____ I feel that I'm making good use of my skills and education in my job.

_____ I think I could make a more significant contribution in some other line of work.

_____ I'd keep my job even if it paid less.

_____ I'd change jobs if I could find one that would provide equal pay and benefits.

_____ I wish I had the skills to do my job better.

_____ I wish I had the skills to find another job.

Looking over the items you checked, do you see a pattern? To what extent do you think your attitude toward your job affects your performance in it? What other factors affect the way you do your work? What's the most important influence on the quality of the work you do? In the remainder of this chapter we will be exploring the importance of the feelings you bring to your role as a care-manager in God's creation.

Differences between Managers and Care-Managers

Christian stewardship involves more than just "managing" as the term is used today. Business as usual isn't good enough for Christian stewards. We are called to go beyond ordinary stewardship to become what I am calling "care-managers." The extra ingredient that distinguishes care-managing from regular managing is *passion* — in the sense of a special emotional involvement, devotion, and zeal. It is the good shepherd's passion for the welfare of the sheep that distinguishes him from the hired hand.

Passion often makes itself evident in an outpouring of activity. Some Christians have an obvious passion for pleasing God and doing God's will. Some people take passionate stands to protect the world and its environment. Passionate devotion inspires some people to provide exceptional leadership to Christ's church as pastors, lay leaders, teachers, and counselors. Just as importantly, passion inspires people to sustain the body of Christ in less obvious ways, by visiting people in jails, hospitals, nursing homes, by preparing meals for people who are ill or down on their luck; even janitors can do their work with passion. A yearning to do God's will transforms our attitude toward everything we do.

As in the case of our attitudes toward our jobs, however, our attitudes toward our role as God's care-managers (stewards) are influenced by many factors. Try to make an honest assessment of which of the following factors motivate you to undertake the responsibility of being a care-manager:

____ obligation   (I am indebted to God or someone else.)

____ fear   (God will punish me if I don't.)

____ reward   (If I give, I'll be paid back for it.)

____ expectations   (My parents/spouse/pastor/etc. expect me to do this.)

____ respect   (I must acknowledge God as ruler of the universe.)

27

____ love   (I want to express my love for God.)

____ partnership   (I want to accept the call to join God in managing the creation.)

____ family   (I am a joint heir with Christ and want to join him in his good work.)

____ awe   (God is so big, and I am so small.)

____ role   (I have accepted Jesus as Lord of my life, and he calls me to be a steward.)

____ rules   (The rules say I should do this.)

____ gratitude   (I'm really thankful and I want to respond.)

____ other   _____

                   _____

Compare the items you checked here with those you checked in the exercise on page 26. Do you see any connections between them? If so, what significance do you think they have? Do you see any further connections to your motives and actions in other areas of life? What about care for the environment, for example? Do you make an effort to conserve and recycle? If so, what motivates you to do so? A sense of obligation, fear for the future if pollution goes unchecked, a desire to preserve the world for our children? What about worship? Do you attend church services out of a sense of duty, out of concern for what others might think, out of habit, out of gratitude to God, in a spirit of anticipation?

We all tend to act as we do in response to a complex set of motivations. Even if our behavior remains, to outward appearances, much the same over time, we typically experience a considerable variety of different motivations. It is scarcely surprising, then, that stewards come in all sizes and shapes, representing many different interests and gifts. This variety is good, because the care-managing needs of God's creation are themselves endlessly varied. In the midst of our differences, we find God encouraging all stewards to work together in love: "Just as I have loved you, you also should love one another. By this everyone will know that you are my disciples, if you have love for one another" (John 13:34b-35).

All Christians are members of God's family, and that provides us with a motivation, too. The One who entrusts all kinds of gifts and responsibilities to us is not a stranger or a boss. We are God's children! We are part of God's family! We enjoy special rights and privileges along with everyone else in God's family. In a more sobering vein, we also have responsibilities. That's what led James Forbes, the pastor of the Riverside Church in New York City, to define stewardship as "living in the Spirit of the Lord." Because we are all members of God's family, he says, Christian stewards want to reflect, resemble, echo, and model the very goodness of the God of the universe.

A Good Example of Care-Managing

Lou George, a denominational executive in Vermont/New Hampshire, is a tither. However, even though he was raised in a Christian home that practiced tithing, he didn't learn to tithe from his parents. Hear the story of how a good care-manager taught him a lot of things about tithing, sharing, and giving:

> My dad died from a heart attack when I was ten years old. My mother had five children to raise, aged seven months to fifteen years, and there was no insurance of any kind. We lived hand to mouth. Making ends meet was tough.
>
> One evening, while I was in eighth grade, I was standing with a group of my friends on a corner in town doing whatever a bunch of normal junior high boys do. As we were talking, a local merchant came down the street to check his store and get a cup of coffee at the restaurant next door. He always stopped to talk with us, to ask us what we were doing and, usually, why we weren't doing something more useful. Before he left, he put his hand on my shoulder and said, "Louie, your mother needs help raising your two younger sisters. You come to work for me on Monday after school." As he walked on toward his school, I said, "Sure, Joe," and we all laughed.
>
> That evening I discussed the conversation with my mother, and she encouraged me to take the job, not so much to help her but to earn some spending money for myself. So, on Monday after school, I showed up at Joe's clothing store and started what was to be four years of work there, at the meager sum of twenty-five cents an hour.
>
> I still remember my first payday. Joe called me to the office for my pay. I was surprised to receive four pay envelopes instead of one. He told me how many hours I had worked and how much money I had earned. Then he handed me the first envelope. It was marked "Tithe." The second envelope

had the word "Savings" written on it. The third was marked "For Your Mother," and the fourth "For Yourself."

I asked him what this was all about. He responded, "If you don't learn how to manage your money when you earn a small amount, you will never learn when you earn a lot." Then he proceeded to explain the envelopes. "I am taking money out of each week's pay to put into a savings account at the bank in your name. I hired you so you could help your mother with your two little sisters, so I've set some aside for her. You need some spending money for yourself, and that's there. But there is also your tithe to your church. I am a Jew — I tithe because the law demands it. You are a Christian — does grace expect any less?"

Joe determined that he would be a care-manager of his young employee Louie. He went far beyond what an ordinary manager would do. He risked offending or alienating a boy who might well have been planning to spend all of his paycheck on himself. But he wanted to help that boy get his priorities in order, and he was successful. As Lou notes today, "The lessons I learned from Joe on my first payday have stayed with me throughout my years of education and Christian ministry. I thank God for a Jewish merchant who cared enough about me to teach me these important life lessons at such a formative stage in my life."

Care-Managing Isn't Necessarily Easy

There is always a price tag attached to any kind of caring. Without question, it takes energy and effort to fill our roles as stewards. Of course, care-managers get help in dealing with the extra burdens and pressure of their role because they work in partnership with God. They are working on God's behalf, and they can derive joy from that fact. This is not to say that they don't run some risk of burnout, however, especially if they try to take too large a share of the partnership onto their own shoulders. Like all other relationships, the relationship between stewards and God calls for balance, for give-and-take.

You may recall the story of Helen Keller. She lost her sight and hearing while she was a baby, and for the next five years she lived in a world of silence and darkness. During that time, she received little discipline. She did what she wanted to do, and she became a little tyrant. Then Annie Sullivan moved into the Keller household to take care of Helen. Annie had both the patience and courage to teach Helen to obey — to sit at the table, to eat properly, to fold her napkin, and the like. Annie gave untold hours of extra time to her task

— not because she was paid but because she saw the tremendous opportunity to unlock the potential in Helen. Annie gave herself to Helen because she cared deeply for this young child with multiple handicaps. In time, Helen began to return her teacher's love. Annie is an excellent example of a care-manager.

I know of a Christian layman whose wife has been hospitalized or in a nursing home for more than five years. In all that time, he hasn't failed to be at her side for a single day. Anyone who has visited people in hospitals and nursing homes will appreciate how exhausting this sort of thing can be. Yet he never complains about the hours he has spent in these places. He's another exceptional example of a care-manager.

In citing these examples, I don't mean to suggest that anyone who fails to do as much as these individuals is somehow deficient in stewardship. Not everyone has the strength or the opportunity or the freedom to be so singularly devoted. But the selflessness and concern that these people evidence are virtues that all of us can aspire to.

If we fail to live up to the obligation we feel to be good stewards, we should not simply give up, any more than we would give up belonging to a family if we disappointed our parents or siblings. Peter denied Jesus in his hour of greatest need, and yet Jesus did not despise or abandon him; he called him to a fresh commitment: "When they had finished breakfast, Jesus said to Simon Peter, 'Simon son of John, do you love me more than these?' He said to him, 'Yes, Lord; you know that I love you.' Jesus said to him, 'Feed my lambs.' A second time he said to him, 'Simon son of John, do you love me?' He said to him, 'Yes, Lord; you know that I love you.' Jesus said to him, 'Tend my sheep.' He said to him the third time, 'Simon son of John, do you love me?' Peter felt hurt because he said to him the third time, 'Do you love me?' And he said to him, 'Lord, you know everything; you know I love you.' Jesus said to him, 'Feed my sheep'" (John 21:15-17). The essence of this rebuke is not an intent to instill guilt but a call to return to service. We should all be motivated to "feed the sheep" by our devotion to Christ and our desire to love him. He calls us to express that love by being good shepherds who care about his sheep.

What Are Christians Care-Managing?

Christian care-managers are the agents of God's plan to give this old world all the tender loving care it can get. The list of things that God has turned over to Christian stewards to care-manage is long. It includes such things as life itself (and specifically the lives of others, such as children and elderly parents), the earth (soil, air, water, and other resources), time, spiritual gifts, money and possessions, the Good News in Jesus Christ (redemption), our neighbors left bruised by the roadside, the congregation of believers, and the very presence of God in our lives through the Spirit of God, who transforms and empowers stewards.

God has expectations of care-managers. The Bible offers suggestions about their conduct: care-managers are expected to be watchful and alert (Luke 12:37), trustworthy (1 Cor. 4:2), and blameless (Tit. 1:7) — not out of some legalistic concern but simply because they are stewards. As care-managers, they reflect what God values most highly — namely, divine grace (Eph. 3:2; Rom. 5:1-2). The challenge we face as Christian stewards is to reflect God on earth to the best of our ability. "Therefore be imitators of God, as beloved children, and live in love, as Christ loved us and gave himself up for us, a fragrant offering and sacrifice to God" (Eph. 5:1-2).

Christian care-managers are God's presence in the world. They may in different times and places emphasize their presence as God's voice, eyes, or feet, but in all of these they are always representatives of God. Care-managers are called upon to be advocates of God's purposes. From this arises the tension of being *in* the world but not *of* the world (see John 17:14-19).

Care-Managing the Good News

God has entrusted the Good News of Jesus Christ to every steward. Some Christians accept this in principle but proceed to act on the assumption that the task of sharing the Good News properly belongs to someone else — to the pastor, to evangelists, to the deacons — to just about anyone other than the person in the pew. But this isn't right. God entrusts the Good News to every person who names the name of Christ and who is willing to stand up and be counted as a Christian. This is not to say that we are all called to be stewards of the Good News in exactly the same manner, but it is to say that we are all called to be stewards in some manner. How do you care-manage the Good News?

The story of the first missionaries to leave the shores of North America reflects a lifelong passion for the Good News. In *To the Golden Shore,* Courtney Anderson relates the story of Adoniram and Ann Judson, missionaries who traveled to the Far East in the early 1800s. During their years in Burma, they witnessed faithfully to anyone who would listen, even to the king. Adoniram was beaten and imprisoned as a result of his efforts. He returned to the United

States only once, many years later. He was in ill health and had lost much of his voice. He found it difficult to address large groups, but one Sunday in the winter of 1846 he decided to try to preach to a congregation in Morrisville, New York.

After the sermon, he spoke for fifteen minutes about his love for Christ, of what he has done for us, and what we owe him in return. The congregation was disappointed. Afterward he was asked why he had not told a story of the mission endeavor.

But, Adoniram responded, "I presented the most interesting subject in the world, to the best of my ability."

"But they wanted a story."

"Well, I am sure I gave them a story . . . the most thrilling one that can be conceived of."

"But they had heard it before. They wanted something new of a man just come from the other side of the world."

"Then I am glad they have it to say, that a man coming [from the other side of the world] had nothing better to tell them than the wondrous story of Jesus' dying love."

The Judsons, and many others before and since, are beautiful illustrations of care-managers with a passion for sharing the Good News of Jesus Christ. Of course, care-managers don't have to go to Burma to express that passion. Each of us can share the Good News in our own Jerusalems (Acts 1:8).

Two Sides to Care-Managing

Jesus provided many illustrations about stewards and their care-managing. Some of them are inspiring stories of faithful stewards who truly cared with a passion. Other stories spell out dire warnings to those who mismanage what God has entrusted to them. Reflect on the following:

Luke 12:16-21	The Parable of the Rich Fool
Luke 16:19-31	The Rich Man and Lazarus
Mark 12:1-12	The Parable of the Wicked Tenants
Luke 17:7-10	We Are Unprofitable Servants
Matthew 20:1-16	The Laborers in the Vineyard
Matthew 25:14-30	The Parable of the Talents
Luke 19:11-28	The Parable of the Pounds
Mark 12:41-44	The Widow's Mite
Luke 15:11-33	The Parable of the Prodigal Son and His Brother

When Kenya handed Angel to me, she was certain that I would be a caring manager. Why? Because of our relationship. Kenya is my granddaughter, but she's even more than that. Several years ago when Kenya was not yet two years old, I had the misfortune of having a broken back. That meant two months in a brace, no sitting or riding in cars, and very limited activity overall. I was most impatient. During this period, Kenya came to live with us for a time. Because of my back problem, I used a makeshift bed in the living room much of the day and evening until it was time to move to the bed upstairs.

At first, Kenya couldn't figure out how to crawl up to sit with me, and I wasn't able to reach down and lift her. But it didn't take her long to figure out how to climb up by herself. So it was that this tiny child sat beside me (sometimes *on* me!) and we talked, read, colored, looked at picture books, or played games together. Sometimes she would put her head on my shoulder and just lay there. I wondered what she was thinking about in this strange set of circumstances. Whatever it was, her love and companionship helped me through a most difficult time. We were inseparable for two months. She cared for me in her little-girl ways. She also managed my life for those long hours each day as she kept a steady supply of toys, books, and attention coming. Even at her age, she was a care-manager — of my life. And she remains a good model. A bond developed between us that will never be broken. She knew I would care for Angel, you see, because I love *her* deeply, and that means I respect the things that are valuable to her. So it is with God and us as stewards. We respond to each other with care because we love each other.

How Is Your Care-Managing?

We all make choices that affect the quality of our care-managing. How are you doing? Jesus stressed the value of faithfulness in stewards. "Whoever is faithful in a very little is faithful also in much," he said; "and whoever is dishonest in a very little is dishonest also in much" (Luke 16:10-11). He also promised that the faithful and wise care-manager will be rewarded. In Matthew 24:45-47, Jesus says that the faithful and wise slave who performs his duties faithfully will be counted blessed by his master and will be given charge over all of the master's belongings.

God is so great and God's love is so boundless that it is often difficult to grasp the full extent of what it really means to be one of Christ's care-managers — joint heirs of the promises of God. Paul summed up the greatness of it all in 1 Corinthians 4:1: "Think of us in this way, as servants of Christ and stewards of God's mysteries." In Romans 16:25-27 we read that the gospel itself was revealed by the command of the eternal God to bring all the nations to faith and obedience. And this is part of our task as well. God provides us with the means whereby we can approach the task: the Holy Spirit within, and the support and stewardship of other obedient disciples without.

Most of us don't often stop to consider the wide spectrum of care-managing expected of us as Christian stewards, but it is good to do so every now and then. So once again: How are you doing? Do you manage with a passion what God has entrusted to you? Are you truly excited about learning all you can about God's hopes and plans for the world and discovering your role in that plan?

List the three things God has entrusted to you that you feel you've been most successful in care-managing:

1. _____

_____

2. _____

_____

3. _____

_____

Now list three things that you've care-managed with only partial success.

1. _____

_____

2. _____

_____

3. _____

_____

Finally, list three things that you haven't made much of an effort to care-manage.

1. _____

_____

2. _____

_____

3. _____

_____

Look over these three lists, pick any two items, and try to come up with some specific ways in which you could improve your care-managing of them.

QUESTIONS FOR DISCUSSION

1. What one thing motivates you more than anything else to try to be one of God's faithful care-managers? If I were to tell you that I didn't feel motivated by the same thing that you do, what would you tell me?

2. It has been said that those passages of the Bible that disturb us the most are often the ones we most need to hear. Which of the passages listed on page 33 disturbs you the most? Why? What connection does this have with your patterns of care-managing?

3. Think of the people you consider to be exceptional care-managers of the Good News of Jesus Christ. What is it that makes them so effective? In what ways do you think it would be possible to emulate them? In what ways would you find it most difficult to emulate them?

4. Have you ever been asked to care-manage something and felt that you were not able to do so? If so, how did you respond? If not, how would you counsel someone else in such a situation?

5. Jesus told the rich young ruler to sell all that he had and then to come and follow him. Is there any sense in which he calls you to do the same? Can you describe any specific ways in which the call to discipleship shapes your care-managing of the money and possessions that have been entrusted to you?

4. Stewardship Is Confronting

*You people . . . are leaders in so many ways — you
have so much faith, so many good preachers, so much
learning, so much enthusiasm, so much love for us.
Now I want you to be leaders also in the spirit of
cheerful giving. I am not giving you an order; I am
not saying you must do it, but others are eager for it.
This is one way to* prove that your love is real, that
it goes beyond mere words.

2 CORINTHIANS 8:7-8,
LIVING BIBLE

The fullness of care-managing is reached when a steward is willing to
become a "confronter" — of self and of others. The willingness to confront is a result of the care-manager's zeal and fervor to do the bidding of the
one who entrusted him or her. As you reflect on your steward's journey, when
was the last time someone confronted you? What was the reason? When was
the last time you confronted someone else, or perhaps even yourself? Have
you ever confronted God? If so, how did you feel about it?

What the Word Confront Really Means

The word *confront* has gotten something of a bad rap in the English language. Most people associate it with opposition, anger, hostility, and threat. Most of us will go out of our way to avoid a confrontation. Who wants to confront a spouse, a neighbor, a coworker, God? Few indeed.

But even if we're not eager for it, we have to admit that confrontation can be necessary sometimes. In some contexts, it might even be unhealthy to avoid it. The root meaning of the word *confront* is actually much softer than is suggested by today's general usage. It simply means "to bring face to face with" or "to come face to face with." This is the key to its positive connotations, and it is in this sense that it should become part of the vocabulary of every Christian steward. Once a Christian has been entrusted with something and is actively involved in care-managing, confrontation naturally takes place.

Confrontation in Everyday Life

Of course, one of the reasons *confrontation* has developed negative associations is that it is part of the meaning of the term that we are brought face to face with things that we are reluctant to face on our own. We speak of being confronted by the truth or confronted by reality, not of being confronted by a compliment or a favorite meal. Some people love waking up in the morning and beginning the daily routine. For some of us, however, staring into a mirror the first thing in the morning amounts to a major confrontation.

I still have strong memories of the birth of our first child just a few days before Christmas. Somehow I wanted our whole family to be together on Christmas Day, and that included our kitten, Fearless. I wanted to surprise my wife, Flossie, and our new baby, Diane, so I snuck Fearless into the hospital in a duffel bag. Needless to say, Flossie at least was surprised! What a moment of excitement just to be together! All was well until a nurse walked in unexpectedly behind me and discovered our secret. She confronted me in no uncertain terms with the rules of the hospital. But then, with a big grin, she said Fearless could stay until I was ready to go. A steady stream of other nurses told us it was fun for them, too. That confrontation wasn't at all bad.

Has a representative of a bank ever confronted you? Sometimes it's confrontation enough just to get your monthly bank statement, bringing you face to face with the reality of your account. Several years ago, our monthly statement showed a sudden increase of $5,000. I showed it to my wife and we laughed about it, knowing we hadn't deposited any such sum in the bank. We had entrusted our money to the bank and assumed they were wise managers in what they did with it. Just for a brief moment, we felt as if we were doing quite well! As you can imagine, we didn't have to do anything about it. The next morning, at 9:00 A.M. sharp, my wife received a call from our bank confronting her with the fact that their computer had made an error. They couldn't be good stewards without bringing us face to face with the reality of their error in our account.

It is a basic part of being a care-manager to be a confronter — faithful, wise, and responsible — on God's behalf. This can be difficult. To carry out this task with integrity, stewards must measure their responsibilities, and the first step in this direction is to be brought face to face with our Creator/Owner God. We confront God through Bible study, dialogue with other Christians, prayer, worship, accepting partnership in God's great plan, and through a variety of life's experiences. In all these ways, we find that care-managing on God's behalf often involves bringing people face to face with reality, truth, hope, solutions, possibilities, injustices, issues, and even life itself. As such, the confronting role is at the heart of the idea of stewardship. From the moment you are entrusted by God with something of value, you will be called on to confront people on God's behalf.

Make a list of people who have confronted you in ways that have changed your behavior, and try to give some indication of what they said or did that got through to you.

1. _____

_____

2. _____

_____

3. _____

_____

4. _____

_____

5. _____

_____

Now make a list of people who confronted you but failed to elicit any change in your behavior, and try to give some indication of why you ignored them.

1. _____

_____

2. _____

_____

3. _____

_____

Confronting in the Old Testament

The first confrontation in the Bible is recorded in the third chapter of Genesis. God confronts Adam and Eve, who had violated their relationship with God by breaking the rules. God's care-managing involved bringing them face to face with the consequences of their actions. Later in Genesis, we find that when Joseph served as chief steward in Egypt, his job demanded that he be a confronter. One of the most beautiful stories of confrontation is found in Genesis 42–45, the story of the separation and reunion of Joseph with his brothers. The climax comes in 45:4-5, where we read how Joseph confronted his brothers with the fact that he was the brother they had sold into slavery in Egypt and then consoled them with the fact that it had all been part of God's plan to preserve their lives and the lives of many others.

Throughout the Old Testament we read that God took the confronter's role again and again. It happened to Moses more than once. The burning bush experience was just one of the times when Moses was brought face to face with God's plans for him. God confronted Samuel as a small boy. God confronted David with reality again and again throughout his life, most dramatically in his experiences with the lion and the bear, Goliath, Saul, Bathsheba, and Absalom.

In addition to confronting individuals personally, God also called people to confront others. For example, God called Moses to confront the Pharaoh of Egypt — not once but many times. Moses dreaded this call, but he responded, repeatedly confronting the Pharaoh with the fact that these slaves were God's people, and he'd better let them go! In Isaiah 6:8 we read that God sought confronters to bring a message to the people: "Then I heard the voice of the Lord saying, 'Whom shall I send, and who will go for us?' And I said, 'Here am I; Send me!'" Verse 9 then states: "And he said, 'Go and say to this people. . . .'" The role of the prophet is to confront. Prophets are entrusted with God's messages about faithfulness, care, and justice. Old Testament prophets brought the Israelites face to face with the reality of God.

Confronting in the New Testament

In Luke 18:18-27 we read that Jesus confronted a wealthy but confused young ruler. The young man wanted to know what he would have to do to "inherit eternal life." Jesus responded somewhat brusquely: "You know the commandments: 'You shall not commit adultery; You shall not murder; You shall not steal; You shall not bear false witness; Honor your father and mother.'" The young man professed that he had kept all these commandments since his youth. Then Jesus brought him face to face with the gap in his devotion to God, with the flaw in his self-assured demeanor: "There is still one thing lacking. Sell all that you own and distribute the money to the poor, and you will have treasure in heaven; then come, follow me." There is a sense in which the young man asked Jesus to confront him with the truth, and yet he had no idea that the truth would be so difficult to deal with. "When he heard this, he became sad; for he was very rich." Jesus knew that the truth would disturb the young man deeply, but he confronted him regardless. In doing so, he was acting as God's steward.

Imagine yourself in a similar situation. Would you be willing to confront the rich young ruler with the truth about his priorities in life. As a more practical matter, are you willing to confront friends as they seek meaning and purpose in life? Are you prepared to bring them face to face with the fact that the true source of happiness in today's world isn't certificates of deposit, bank accounts, pension funds, life insurance policies, or lottery winnings? Are you willing to suggest, as tactfully and carefully as possible, that seeking God is the highest priority for the Christian steward?

At the time of Christ's ascension, recorded in Acts 1:1-11, Jesus stated, "You will receive power when the Holy Spirit has come upon you; and you will be my witnesses" — that is to say, you will bring others face to face with the gospel — "in Jerusalem, in all Judea and Samaria, and to the ends of the earth" (v. 8). We know how high a value God places on the world from the Good News that God has sent into it (John 3:16). Christian stewards are called to be God's managers of the Good News and bring people and institutions face to face with the gospel.

Acts 4:5-12 tells us how Peter confronted the rulers, elders, and scribes of Jerusalem with the reality of the living Christ. He charged them with having rejected the stone — Jesus — that God had designated to become the chief cornerstone. Of course, Jesus himself reminded Peter that he had not always been so staunch a supporter and ally. We have already noted the confrontation recorded in John 21:15-17, in which the risen Lord alluded to Peter's denial on the eve of the crucifixion. At that point, far from confronting other people with the truth, Peter was himself evading the truth, running from it, edging away from the light into the darkness. But that was not the end of the story: Peter found forgiveness and redemption and returned to witness to the truth, to confront others with it. We all struggle, like Peter, in taking on the confronter's role. There will be moments when, for any of a number of reasons, we will choose to avoid a confrontation, we will run from truth and confrontation; but, with the help of God, we will find occasions on which we can courageously and enthusiastically confront ourselves and others with the truth of the Good News.

Confronting Today

In the days of the early church, Paul, Peter, John, and others devoted a good deal of energy to bringing Christians face to face with who and what God wanted them to be. God confronts our local churches today in the same way. Get a copy of your congregation's purpose or mission statement. This document should clearly spell out your church's reason for being *today* — not many years ago. Is your congregation a living example of what God has called it to be? God asks all congregations to be exemplary stewards of what has been entrusted to them.

The church of today needs to define a vision of its confronter's role as much today as at any time in history. The standards and values in our society are constantly shifting, and selfless modeling is in short supply. The church needs to become more involved in lovingly and caringly bringing people face to face with the reality of the gospel of Jesus Christ.

In what ways is your congregation confronting people today? Think about its place in the community in and to which you minister. Go through the following list of various groups of people and try to be specific in describing the ways in which your church is confronting them.

Unchurched _____

_____

Poor _____

_____

Hurting _____

_____

Lonely _____

_____

Homeless _____

_____

Illiterate _____

_____

Unemployed _____

_____

Hospitalized _____

_____

Handicapped _____

_____

Elderly _____

_____

Prisoners _____

_____

Students _____

_____

Politicians _____

_____

There is also a need for a good deal of healthy confrontation within congregations. One of the areas in which confrontation is appropriate is the matter of giving. My brother and I were born during the Great Depression, and our family was among the poorest of the poor. When we made the decision to follow Christ, our pastor boldly confronted us with the fact that we were now expected to be tithers. We weren't familiar with the concept, but he patiently explained. Still, our family often wondered where the next meal would come from. How could we be expected to tithe? My brother and I received an allowance of a nickel a week at that time. How were we supposed to tithe that? Our pastor had an answer: we could put a penny in the envelope every two weeks. He was quite serious. It's wasn't much money to give to God, maybe, but we knew its value nonetheless. We knew that the nine cents we had left couldn't buy what the dime would. At our young ages, we were effectively brought face to face with the reality of tithing. Our pastor did not hesitate to give boxes of envelopes to us. Neither did he hide the fact that he and his wife were also tithers. As a result, I have never forgotten his teaching or modeling, nor have I ceased to tithe.

It has never been easy for Christians to come face to face with the realities of the gospel. Many of us do not want to face anything that involves change, disruption, or sacrifice. In the pulpit and the pew as much as anywhere else, we prefer comfort to discomfort. There is a temptation in our churches today to stress the fact that Jesus sought peace almost to the exclusion of the fact that he sought justice. Such a distortion of the gospel is dangerous. One need only read Matthew to know that justice was a burning concern of Christ. He challenged his followers, now as then, to address injustices. In responding to the obligations of stewardship, we must be willing to assume the risks of confronting others with the issues, concerns, and challenges associated with change. As the saying goes, if you seek peace, you must work for justice.

Let's return to the subject of giving for a minute. The possibility of a confrontation exists every time the subject of an offering is raised. An appeal for funds always brings us face to face with the fact that we are only care-managers of what belongs to God. Whatever the reason for the appeal, it becomes a problem if someone suggests how much we ought to give. Most North Americans feel strongly that how much we give is our own business. As a result, in our churches most people have little idea what anyone else gives. The young have no models, nor do new Christians. Congregations spend far more time protecting the anonymity of givers than they do in providing models or giving counsel for others to follow. Why do we hesitate to confront one another with the fact that we should be returning at least a tithe to the God who has supplied us with all good things?

It is the task of each of us as Christian stewards to confront the fact that we are called to responsible stewardship and to encourage all of our brothers and sisters in Christ to do the same. Sometimes we need models; sometimes we have to serve as models ourselves. We can present a powerful witness by saying publicly, "I am a tither, and it is good." During a visit to the Philippines in the 1970s, A. Q. Van Benschoten Jr., a former Baptist missionary to Thailand, noted that many of the churches placed a list of their members in the narthex, and alongside each name was a record of how much he or she had given! Stop a moment and evaluate the pros and cons of that approach.

Some churches provide public opportunities for members to share their personal stories and adventures in tithing or other forms of sharing. Less overt kinds of confronting take place constantly in church as well. A twenty-six-year-old law student told me of having visited a church in South Dakota and being shocked by seeing a ten dollar bill in the offering plate. All his life he had assumed that no one ever put more than a dollar into the offering plate when it was passed. He admitted to being confronted by the reality of his obligation to help sustain the life and ministry of his congregation, and he decided his giving pattern had to change.

Jesus lived what he taught and preached. He didn't just talk about giving: he healed, comforted, instructed, hoped, encouraged, provided a vision, and even gave his life (John 10:15, 17). The words at the beginning of this chapter, from 2 Corinthians 8:7-8, remind us that we are called to adopt a spirit of cheerful giving, to demonstrate in tangible ways that our love is real, "that it goes beyond mere words." Paul's selflessness afforded him opportunities to bring others face to face with the obligation to be selfless. The combination of doing and exhorting is probably the most effective means by which we, too, might confront others with the same obligation.

Chief Stewards Are Chief Confronters

Among the spiritual gifts that God has promised to provide to the church is leadership. In most of our congregations the clergy and lay leaders serve as our chief stewards — and hence our chief confronters. Though modeling is not limited to leaders, they often provide our most visible examples. In many cases, a congregation can learn most effectively when it is brought face to face with biblical stewardship through the way its leaders live out the mandate.

Consider the prayer of St. Francis of Assisi: "Lord, make us instruments of thy peace. Where there is hatred, let us sow love; where there is injury, pardon; where there is discord, union; where there is doubt, faith; where there is despair, hope; where there is darkness, light; where there is sadness, joy." To be instruments of God's peace, we must be confronters. To sow love where there is hatred will involve bringing people face to face with the need for God's peace. Where there is injury, discord, doubt, despair, and darkness, there must be change, and we are called to be instruments of that change.

The prophet Micah long ago laid down a guideline for authentic religious behavior when he asked, "What does the LORD require of you but to do justice, and to love kindness, and to walk humbly with your God?" (Mic. 6:8).

Sharon Parks tells the true story of a six-year-old girl who had been shuttled from one to another of a long line of foster homes. As she was being tucked into bed by her latest foster mother, she surprised the woman by asking her to take off her wedding ring so she could see it. Wanting to respond warmly to the little girl, she did as requested. She was startled when the little girl clutched the ring tightly and put her little fist firmly under her pillow. "There," she said. "Now you won't leave me while I'm sleeping."

The child was a confronter. In one small but powerful act, she brought her new foster mother face to face with the reality of her feelings about life — her cycles of faith and doubt, promise and betrayal, power and powerlessness, belonging and exclusion, hope and suffering. In the end, the little girl just didn't want to be left alone again. At least for one night, she dared to confront.

As members of the church of Jesus Christ, we are all called to confront. Whether that means introducing someone to Christ, supplying food for the hungry, dealing with teens on alcohol and drugs, dealing with those who sell the drugs to them, providing housing for the homeless, sharing love with abused children, or working to save our environment, we are called to responsible stewardship.

QUESTIONS FOR DISCUSSION

1. List three ways in which God has called you to be a more responsible Christian steward. What means has God used to confront you, and how have you responded?

2. Many Christians in our culture feel awkward about confronting strangers with the truth of the gospel of Jesus Christ and prefer to express their stewardship in other ways, such as by giving money to mission causes. Do you feel that every Christian has an obligation to make a personal

witness to others, or are some Christians justified in restricting their stewardship to other areas?

3. Think of some recent experiences in which you have been confronted by someone else, and recall especially the things that you most resented and appreciated about these confrontations. With this in mind, can you think of any specific ways in which you might more effectively confront someone else?

4. If friends of yours expressed a desire to become more caring, confronting managers of what God has entrusted to them, what suggestions could you offer them?

5. In what ways has God confronted your congregation to be more responsible Christian stewards? How has your congregation responded?

6. Is your congregation currently involved in any efforts to help your community come face to face with God's plan for humanity? If so, what do you think are the most effective means you are employing, and what more might be done along these lines? If not, what do you think it would take to make this happen, and what would you be willing to do to help?

5. Stewardship of Money and Possessions: Tithing . . . and Beyond

Each of you must give as you have made up your mind, not reluctantly or under compulsion, for God loves a cheerful giver.

2 CORINTHIANS 9:7

Stewardship of Money and Possessions

Stewardship encompasses all of life. In our culture, money and possessions figure as a not inconsiderable part of life. I know that money is a touchy subject for a lot of people, and some of what we encounter in this chapter may well stimulate some tensions. Nevertheless, it is time to confront directly the issues of money and possessions and how Christians deal with them.

Some church members think of stewardship narrowly as a matter of obtaining and managing funds and properties of the church. The Bible gives us many indications, however, that our stewardship of money involves far more than the maintenance of the church's buildings and resources. In our records of his ministry, Jesus speaks more about money and possessions than about any other subject. He knew that money could easily become a barrier between people, as well as between people and God.

Money played a role in Jesus' life on a daily basis. The only named position in his small group of twelve disciples was that of treasurer. And, ironically, it was this treasurer who eventually betrayed him — for a sum of money, thirty pieces of silver.

Not a few scholarly tomes have been dedicated to the subject of the stewardship of money and possessions. In this brief chapter, our survey will necessarily be limited. We will proceed by (1) taking a brief look at what the Bible says about money and possessions, (2) focusing on some of Jesus' teachings and attempting to connect them with our lives today, (3) studying the concept of the lordship of Jesus, (4) considering the practice of tithing, (5) addressing the question of how much we should give, and (6) looking at some steps churches can take to help Christians be better stewards of money and possessions.

Biblical Teachings about Money and Possessions

The Old Testament contains many references to money and possessions. The concept of stewardship was an integral part of their history. Tithing — that is, giving one-tenth of their wealth to God — was a way of life for the Hebrews. The Old Testament also contains instructions for giving a portion of the firstfruits of each harvest to God and making additional contributions through such practices as the cancellation of debt in sabbatical years (i.e., every seventh year) and even more extravagant measures to banish poverty and hardship in Jubilee years (i.e., every fiftieth year).

Tithing is first referred to in Genesis 28:22, where an offering of the spoils of war is described. The command to tithe appears in Leviticus 27:30. More instruction concerning the tithe can be found in Numbers 18:26 and Deuteronomy 14:22-29. God's people tithed fields, grains, flocks, herds, money, and even people!

Proverbs 3:9 speaks of giving the firstfruits to God: "Honor the LORD with your substance, and with the first fruits of all your produce." The firstfruits of a harvest are usually the biggest and best. The Hebrews were expected to give their best to God — the cream off the top. Today, our firstfruits might include our freshest efforts, the prime hours of our day, our quality time, a portion of our wages before taxes, a dedication of our best skills, and the like.

Leviticus 25 records the establishment of the year of Jubilee. Every fiftieth year, the land was to be left fallow so that it might regain vigor, all outstanding debts were to be canceled, the people who had been forced to sell themselves into indentured servitude to pay debts were to be set free, and all property was to revert to the original titleholder as a lesson that all property ultimately belongs to God and his people are only sojourners in the land he provides. Basically, then, the Jubilee year gave impoverished people the opportunity to start over with a clean slate, and it gave those who were doing all right the opportunity to reflect on the needs of others and then to do something about them.

In New Testament times, money and possessions were just as much an issue as they are today. Jesus was not rich, certainly, but neither is there any evidence that he came from an especially poor background. He was a carpenter, and in that day people who worked at trades usually earned an adequate living. Jesus made many statements about money. Among the best known are "No slave can serve two masters. . . . You cannot serve God and wealth" (Luke 16:13) and "Give to everyone who begs from you, and do not refuse anyone who wants to borrow from you" (Matt. 5:42).

The New Testament also includes much about money and wealth outside the four Gospels, such as the passage from 2 Corinthians that appears at the beginning of this chapter and the following verse from the book of Hebrews: "Keep your lives free from love of money, and be content with what you have" (13:5). See also James 1:9-10; 2 Timothy 3:1-5; 1 Peter 4:10; and 2 Corinthians 8:2-4.

The ideas about money and sharing that Paul presents in 2 Corinthians 8 challenge and set the tone for those who are Christ's followers. Paul insists that the work of Christ is to be supported by those who are "members of his body" — that is, members of the church. He summarizes much of the thinking of the day regarding wealth in 1 Timothy 6:17-19: "As for those who in the present age are rich, command them not to be haughty, or to set their hopes on the uncertainty of riches, but rather on God who richly provides us with everything for our enjoyment. They are to do good, to be rich in good deeds, generous, and ready to share, thus laying up for themselves the treasure of a good foundation for the future, so that they may take hold of the life that really is life."

Paul became a fund-raiser during his ministry, though probably not by choice. Then, as now, many people with financial resources were reluctant to share and found excuses not to give. Paul challenged these people to give regularly, and indeed to give beyond their means. He told them to give of themselves first and then to give of their money. He received a fair amount of criticism for his fund-raising zeal and generated some hostility, so we can safely conclude that he wasn't always successful in his efforts to persuade potential donors to give.

At the heart of all of the Bible's instructions regarding our relationship to money and possessions is the image of a very loving and generous God who not only supplies us with all that we have but who has made the ultimate sacrifice on our behalf on the cross. Those who follow Christ are called upon to reflect this love and generosity. Again and again, the Bible reminds us that God wants us to give of ourselves, to love as we have been loved, to give as it has been given to us. It is the Christian way to give because we love, even as God loved . . . and then gave.

Jesus' Teachings and How They Speak to Us Today

Jesus calls his followers to share, to respond to the poor, the hungry, the destitute, the homeless, the widowed, the prisoners. To one inquiring young man he said, "If you wish to be perfect, go, sell your possessions, and give the money to the poor, and you will have treasure in heaven; then come, follow me" (Matt. 19:21). Much of what Jesus said about money and possessions stood in striking contrast to common practice and to what people wanted to hear, both then and now! Many of Jesus' parables focus on the stewardship of resources.

In capsule form, here are some of Jesus' views concerning money and possessions:

- He encouraged giving: "It is more blessed to give than to receive."
- He himself provided a model for sharing.
- He advocated making special efforts to care for the poor and destitute.
- He most likely gave more than a tithe himself, but he didn't preach the tithe.
- He was far less concerned about the amount a person gave than about the spirit that lay behind the giving — as in the case of the widow's mite.
- He recommended simple values.
- He taught that treasures in heaven are more important than treasures on earth.
- He was completely committed to the belief that God is the owner of everything.
- He condemned ostentatious giving.
- He gave out of love.

Recall the distinction we made in Chapter 1 between the ownership model, which is centered in the idea that my possessions belong to me, and the biblical model, which is centered in the idea that everything belongs first of all to God and that we are to serve as stewards of God's wealth, giving help to one another as we are able. The models envision two very different sorts of worlds and call for very different approaches to money and possessions.

Our attitude toward money is necessarily tempered by our concept of ownership. If we believe that all we possess has been entrusted to us by God and that we are to manage it on God's behalf, we will have a much easier time negotiating Jesus' teachings in this area than we will if we remain committed to a "getting and keeping" vision of ownership.

Many people in our culture are made uncomfortable by Jesus' strong and highly judgmental comments about those who have wealth. In Luke 6:24-25 we read that he said, "But woe to you who are rich, for you have received your consolation. Woe to you who are full now, for you will be hungry. Woe to you who are laughing now, for you will mourn and weep." The people in our society own more things, have more food, and are more entertained than almost any other people in history. We have reason to be concerned that Jesus is saying woe to us.

One brief news item rather quickly summarizes much of what we deal with today. A few years ago the Associated Press ran a story about Dr. Darold Treffert of the Winnebago (Wisconsin) Mental Health Institute, who presented the argument that North American teenagers were being victimized by what he called "the American Fairy Tale." The story read in part:

Amy, 15, had always gotten straight "As" in school, and her parents were extremely upset when she got a "B" on her report card. "If I fail in what I do," Amy wrote her parents, "I fail in what I am." The message was part of Amy's suicide note.

"The American Fairy Tale," said Treffert, "begins with two themes: that more possessions mean more happiness, that a person who does or produces more is more important."

In so many words, we frequently hear people asking, "What's in it for me?" Self-interest is near the top of our culture's list of priorities. Efforts to protect our global environment, for example, are often elbowed out of the way by concerns to protect corporate profits, personal comfort, and a short-term bottom line.

In so many words, we frequently hear people saying, "It's mine, and I can do whatever I want with it." There seems to be general agreement that possession is nine-tenths of the law, that our homes are our castles, and that it amounts to a violation of basic human rights to question what anyone else does with anything he or she holds title to.

Since we can't fully separate ourselves from our culture, the question remains how we as Christians should apply the teachings of Christ to our use of money today. We have to start by refamiliarizing ourselves with what it is that Christ taught. We won't find any pat answers, but we can find a wealth of guidelines in the recorded sayings of Jesus and elsewhere in the books of the New Testament. Today's churches need to grapple with these guidelines more earnestly than we are doing now. We must educate ourselves and one another and then act on what we have found to provide living models of stewardship for one another.

What conclusions begin to emerge? Is money in and of itself evil? Money builds hospitals and provides medicine. Money fills community pantries and keeps shelters for the homeless in operation. Properly used, money can give hope when hope is gone. But money also fuels the traffic in illegal drugs, funds the construction of countless weapons of mass destruction, and is squandered on accumulations of shameful luxuries. The great Methodist preacher John Wesley said, "The fault lies not in the money, but in them that use it. It may be used ill; and what may not?" In the same context, Wesley gave his classic formula for those engaged in business activities: "1. Gain all you can; 2. Save all you can; 3. Give all you can."

Jesus made many strong statements about what God expects of those who would be his children. The one thing that seems clear regarding questions about a Christian's relationship to money and possessions is that they are all secondary to a more basic life question: "Who is this Christ, and how does he want me to live my life today?" The disciples responded to this question by turning their lives over to the risen, glorified Christ. Paul faced the question on the Damascus Road, crying out, "Who are you, Lord?" He committed the rest of his life to sharing the Good News throughout his world. Christians today need to ask the same basic question, and the answer they find will determine their response to questions about money and possessions.

Acknowledging Jesus as Lord

"When I was a child," wrote Paul, "I spoke like a child, I thought like a child, I reasoned like a child; when I became an adult, I put away childish things" (1 Cor. 13:11). A number of passages in the Bible indicate that all Christians are expected to grow spiritually, and yet many seem content to live in a kind of endless childhood. Spiritual growth is a fundamental component of good stewardship, and in order to grow we need a clear understanding of authority. In 1 Thessalonians, Jesus is called "Lord." This is the New Testament equivalent of the Old Testament's "Yahweh," often rendered LORD in our English translations. Both terms connote authority.

In Jesus' time, "Lord" was the title by which slaves referred to their masters. The Romans also used the term, greeting each other with the phrase "Caesar is Lord." The response was, "He is Lord indeed." After Jesus' ascension, the early Christians altered this Roman phrase to declare "Jesus is Lord." Can't you just hear their enthusiastic responses — "He is Lord indeed!" Lest we forget, many of the early Christians were put to death because they refused to say that Caesar was their Lord. To do so would have been a denial of their confession of faith, for they knew that the slave can serve only one master.

In his book *The Mind of Jesus,* William Barclay summarizes his thinking about the lordship of Jesus. "When I call Jesus Lord," he says, it ought to mean that

- "he is the absolute and undisputed owner and possessor of my life" — which is to say that we belong to him, body and soul;
- "he is the Master, whose servant and slave I must be all my life long" — which is to say that we have elected to serve as his stewards;
- "I think of him as the head of that great family in heaven and on earth of which God is the Father, and of which I through him have become a member" — which is to say that we are alike children of God and brothers and sisters to all of God's other children;
- "I think of him as the help of the helpless and the guardian of those who have no other to protect them" — which is to say that he serves as a model to us in showing love to those who need it most;
- "I look on him as having absolute authority over all my life, all my thoughts, all my actions" — and this includes our ambitions, our relationships, our priorities, and our possessions;
- "he is the King and Emperor to whom I owe and give my constant homage, allegiance and loyalty" — and we pledge to seek first the kingdom of God in our personal and professional lives, in social and community life, and in national and global contexts; and
- "for me he is the Divine One whom I must ever worship and adore" — and this above all else, to the exclusion of any pretender to the throne.

Do you call Jesus Lord? If so, what does it mean to you to do so?

Underlying Reasons for Giving and Sharing

Why do you give the amount of money you give? To help find an answer to that question, it may be useful to take a closer look at your motivations in giving. Look over the list that follows and check all the items that you feel motivate you in some way.

Reasons for Giving

____ a desire to help others

____ a deep love for God and God's gifts to me

____ I have more than I need to take care of myself and those who depend on me

____ to fund special projects/programs that are important to me

____ to do my share in meeting the expenses of my congregation

____ to spread the gospel around the world

____ to meet people's special needs

____ it feels good

____ because Jesus Christ is Lord of my life

____ to relieve feelings of guilt

____ because I learned to do it as a child

____ to pay something back to God

____ because it affects what others think about me

____ to obey Jesus

____ because Jesus gave his life for me

____ it is a habit

____ a desire to control those who receive what I give

____ it's the thing to do

____ because someone I love insists that I do so

____ because I have been asked to do so

____ because I *need* to give

____ to receive tax credits

____ because it's good business

____ because those who give receive in turn

____ other

Most of us are motivated to give by a considerable number of different factors, some appropriate and others less so. Looking over this list, can you think of any ways in which the relative importance of the various motivations you experience has changed over time as you have grown spiritually? Can you think of any ways in which the church promotes less appropriate motivations for giving? Can you think of any ways in which your brothers and sisters in Christ could help you to approach giving in more appropriate ways?

In his book *Creative Stewardship,* Richard Cunningham offers some thoughts on biblical principles of motivation for giving. You may find them helpful as you wrestle with the question of how much you should give. Circle the numbers beside those principles that motivate you at the present time.

1. Give as a response to God's grace (2 Cor. 8:7).
2. Give as a response to the example of Christ, who gave himself for us (2 Cor. 8:9).
3. Give as a response to human need (Luke 10:29-37).
4. Give as an expression of thanksgiving to God (2 Cor. 9:12).
5. Give as a form of sacrifice to God (Phil. 4:18).
6. Give as a way of symbolizing your commitment of all of your resources to the service of God and others (1 Cor. 6:20).
7. Give as a concrete proof of love (2 Cor. 8:8, 24).

Since the spirit in which we give is as important as the amount we give, consider Cunningham's suggestions on procedures for giving.

1. Put first things first (Matt. 6:33).
2. Give of the self before any material gift (2 Cor. 8:5).
3. Give God the first and best you possess (Exod. 22:29; Mal. 1:6).
4. Give voluntarily (2 Cor. 8:3; 9:5).
5. Give proportionately as God prospers you (2 Cor. 8:12).
6. Give generously (2 Cor. 8:2; 9:11).

7. Give spontaneously (Matt. 6:2-4).
8. Give sacrificially (Luke 21:3-4).
9. Give systematically (1 Cor. 16:2).
10. Give humbly (Matt. 6:1-4).
11. Give in love (1 Cor. 13:3).

Tithing . . . and Beyond

From the beginning, the people of God have struggled with the question of how much they should give to God and to others. Many Christians wrestle all their lives with the question without finding an answer that satisfies. Some Christians establish a standard of giving and maintain it throughout their lives. Others keep searching for new and different ways to give.

Some Christians give generously of their time but have little money to give. Some give generous financial gifts but are hesitant to get personally involved in any sort of ministry. The clear message of the Bible, however, is that we are called both to give and to serve. As one Christian leader said, "Show me your calendar and your checkbook, and I can write your biography. I will know how you spend your time and your money; that constitutes your treasure."

The subject of tithing lies at the heart of the Christian's struggle to answer the question about how much to give. Jesus didn't stress tithing; neither did Paul. By the time of Jesus' ministry, the practice of tithing was assumed in Israel. In Matthew 23:23, we read that Jesus acknowledged that the scribes and Pharisees had been scrupulous about their tithing and granted that they were right not to neglect such matters, but he implicitly indicated that these were lesser matters in the greater scheme of things: "Woe to you, scribes and Pharisees, hypocrites! For you tithe mint, dill, and cummin, and have neglected the weightier matters of the law: justice and mercy and faith. It is these you ought to have practiced without neglecting the others." Thus Jesus calls us to a more expansive discipleship, to do more than just what the law demands — and yet this does not mean that we should abandon our concern about the more mundane aspects of the law, such as tithing in our daily lives. As Irenaeus, Bishop of Lyons, put it, "Jesus did not abolish the tithe, but put it into a deeper meaning." His primary concern was not just keeping rules but seeking and doing God's will, whatever that might entail.

There are several other explanations for Jesus' lack of emphasis on the tithe. One of the clearest may be the anger, hurt, and frustration that was commonly associated with the tithe during the time of Christ and Paul. In his book *The Wealth of Christians,* Redmund Mullin has given a careful account of giving and what it was like to be Jewish at the time of Christ:

> Taxes and tithes for the support of temple or priests were not regarded as charity. The Heave offering (a portion of the harvest) was to be eaten only by the priests. Every competent adult male was to pay a half-shekel annually to the temple. Additionally, there were three tithes: the first was for the Levite, who was in his turn to give a tithe of the tithe to the priest; the second was to be consumed in Jerusalem, unless a corresponding sum of money was sent to Jerusalem (this tithe was in part a form of relief for the poor in the city); the third tithe was for the poor, and replaced the Levitical tithe in the third and sixth years of each seven-year cycle.

All this and more was expected of the Jews. Altogether, these requirements soaked up well beyond thirty percent of their income. Given this state of affairs, neither Jesus nor Paul felt the tithe was an effective guide for giving. Instead, they called people to give more than they thought they could. The New Testament provides us with examples of people who gave far more than tithe: Zaccheus gave fifty percent; the widow who gave the mite, one hundred percent. Jesus clearly taught that everything we have comes from God, and we are responsible to manage everything according to God's priorities. Paul suggested that we should give according to the level of our prosperity. Jesus expected much more than that. He established a new commandment of giving of self, breaking the old legalistic patterns of giving.

The tithe was a complicated, costly matter, and yet Jesus did not advocate abandoning it. At the same time, however, he had no intention of perpetuating a system built on laws (e.g., you must give ten percent — no less, no more). It was Jesus' hope that his followers would be generous and spontaneous givers, not bound by the limits of a fixed percentage. He challenged his followers to give their lives for others. A ten percent standard pales in comparison with what Jesus calls his followers to give!

Throughout the Old Testament, we find the theme of God's love for those made "a little lower than the angels" (Ps. 8:5, KJV). In the New Testament, there is no question that love is at the center of all of Jesus' life and activity. The New Testament is the story of the fullness of God's love expressed in and through the person of Jesus. Jesus' love was complete. He gave everything he possessed — including his life. When he died on the cross, he was totally devoid of possessions. Why was he willing to give in this manner? Because he loved God, and he loved a sinful, hurting, fallen humanity enough to reopen a door to God for them by being the sacrifice. Dollars and cents, possessions, and tithes pale in comparison with what Jesus gave.

The essence of God is love, and God's gift of Christ came from the center of that love. Jesus gave his life because he loved us. If we, as Christians, are to reflect our loving and wonderful God and also our loving, crucified, and resurrected Savior, then should not love be the basis for what we give? This type of giving goes beyond percentages, pledges, tax deductions, and all the other motivations for giving found in our culture and economic systems. It is love that produces sacrificial giving.

Do you know anyone who gives sacrificially? Such people are fairly rare in our culture because it is not an easy thing to develop a pure love for God and one another in the midst of a consumer society. Gilbert Davis, a recently retired director of church relations at Texas Christian University in Fort Worth, has related a couple of stories illustrating biblical reasons for giving and tithing.

Several years ago, Gilbert gave a speech about ministerial education to a group of church women in Dallas. At the end of the speech, a woman came to him and said, "The next time you are in Dallas, would you come by and visit me? I would like to talk with you about an important matter." It was only a few days later that he and a coworker took the opportunity to make their way to her humble home in a modest section of the city.

We knocked on the door. This good woman met us, ushered us through the living room into the kitchen. We had a cup of coffee and a marvelous visit. After a while, she said, "I am about to do something very important. Would one of you lead us in prayer?" I offered a prayer. Then she said, "I want to make a gift of $10,000 to Brite Divinity School." Now, we looked all around that house, and there wasn't anything in it that looked like $10,000. We knew the woman was of sound mind, and meant to do what she said, and had the wherewithal to do it. Ed said, "I assume you have other resources." "Oh, yes, I get a Social Security check every month, and I supplement it by working as a serving lady in the Highland Park Cafeteria." I said to her, "But suppose you had an extended illness, or you needed to be in a nursing home for a long time." She said, "My father left me this ten thousand dollars; I have never needed it. God loves me and has always taken care of me. I'm sure he always will. I want to invest this money in the Kingdom." We talked long and hard to persuade her to put the item in her will, which was more appropriate than an outright gift. As we left her house that day, I said to her, "You are a generous woman." She responded, "God has been generous with me."

Gilbert loves to tell this tithing story to illustrate that no matter how much you have, if you love and trust God, you can tithe.

Gilbert also relates a story he heard from his friend Bishop Bob Goodrich. In his first week as pastor of the Trinity Methodist Church in El Paso, Texas, Goodrich received a thick envelope through the mail. Inside he found seven little envelopes, each containing seventy-five cents. Across each of them were written the words "My tithe." An accompanying letter read, "Dear Pastor, I am no longer able to attend church because of poor health, but here is my tithe," and it was signed "Joe Prime." Goodrich asked the church secretary to tell him about Joe Prime. "He's a victim of tuberculosis," she explained, "living in a little lean-to shack, back of a big house in a very poor section of El Paso. He lives on a pension of seven dollars and a half a week. He is able to stay in that house because a Christian nurse comes by every morning and prepares his food from a little refrigerator on a hot plate for the day." Goodrich went to visit Joe, and he reported that, as he stood at his bedside, he felt he was standing in the presence of spiritual royalty.

A month or so later, during the Christmas season, another envelope came to the church office. This time it was from a serviceman who enclosed a check for a hundred dollars to the church. He wrote, "Pastor, I want fifty dollars to go to the church budget and fifty dollars to help somebody in our congregation to have a good Christmas." Goodrich immediately thought of Joe Prime and went to see the old fellow.

"Brother Prime," he said, "I have good news for you this morning. I've brought you a Christmas present."

"What is it?"

"One of our more fortunate members has made me his ambassador to bring you good news, a Christmas greeting, and a check for fifty dollars."

The old fellow's face lit up, and tears began to flow down his cheeks. "Pastor, you don't know how happy this makes me," he said. "Every year at Christmas our church has two special offerings — one for the orphanage and one for missions. I never have any money. I give my tithe, but don't have any more money. This year I am going to give twenty-five dollars to the orphanage and twenty-five dollars to missions."

"But Brother Joe," said Goodrich, "you don't understand. This is for your Christmas. You give your tithe."

"The greatest joy I could have this Christmas is to be able to make those two gifts," said Joe. The gifts were made.

Seven years later, Goodrich left El Paso to come to Dallas. Two or three weeks later, he received a letter from the church secretary informing him that one day the past week, the Christian nurse went over to prepare Joe Prime's breakfast and discovered that in the night the old fellow had gone to a better country. But there by the bedside were two little offering envelopes containing seventy-five cents each. Each bore the words "My tithe." "His master said to him, 'Well done, good and trustworthy slave; you have been trustworthy in a few things, I will put you in charge of many things; enter into the joy of your master'" (Matt. 25:21).

As we seek to determine how we should give, we need some sort of standard, some sort of guide. This standard should take into account our unique faith journey, circumstances, and commitments.

For myself, I begin with the standard of the tithe, and then go as far beyond it as I can. If you have not already established your own standard, you should begin by negotiating with God, in consultation with the Bible and others of the faith. If your means do not permit, you need not begin with a ten percent standard; you can establish whatever level of giving is realistic and reflects a degree of sacrificial giving. For some that may be two percent; for others it could be twenty-two percent. I strongly believe we should all review our level of giving at least annually, though we should not become so much a slave to a yearly review that we rule out increasing our commitment in special circumstances at any time. One of the great blessings of being part of a community of believers is that God hears and responds to the prayers of those who can give only small amounts as well as those who are able to give larger amounts.

In his book *The Tithe: Legalism or Challenge*, Douglas W. Johnson speaks to the concept of tithing in a specifically affluent society:

> First, the tithe is not an appropriate standard for giving in an affluent society. The tithe is a rather easy rule to follow and, by following it, the more stringent demands of giving are ignored. . . . Second, God's demands are far greater than the tithe, a 10% token of one's possessions.
>
> Third, the tithe, for an affluent Christian, holds no opportunity for sacrifice. . . . The tithe in an affluent society is no more than a charitable deduction. . . . Fourth, the tithe talks only about money. Giving should not be tied only to money.

Tithing has often been misinterpreted and misunderstood. Many in the church view it as a legalistic requirement. Some consider it a burdensome duty rather than an opportunity for the joyful expression of praise. Some view tithing as an investment, assuming that the more they give, the more they'll get. Some see tithing as a requisite proof of redemption, as a sort of good work that is exacted as the price of salvation. For those who hold such a perspective, either consciously or unconsciously, tithing can become very problematic: they experience guilt if they feel they may not have given enough, and they become complacent or even arrogant if they feel they have contributed lavishly. We pervert the concept of the tithe if we imagine ten percent to be a magic number that guarantees some kind of relationship with God.

If we focus too narrowly on a specific percentage, we wind up tangled in all manner of details. Do we tithe net or gross income? Do contributions to charities count as part of the tithe? These are not irrelevant issues as such — we do well to give some thought to how we assess the gifts that we have been given and which ministries are worthy of our support — but the point is that if we are looking to cut our losses when it comes to tithing, then we have got it all wrong. Legalistic interpretations can quickly kill the spirit of gratitude that should be motivating us to tithe in the first place. We should approach tithing as an expression of Christian grace, not as a device for earning redemption. Tithing is a response — not a requirement. The progression of stewardship toward and beyond the tithe can be a discipline that frees us to comprehend the fullness of the gospel and the riches of God's grace. Properly handled, tithing is a vital step in Christian discipleship.

The essential points to keep in mind with regard to tithing are the following:

- Everything we have is from God.
- We are called to be good stewards of all that God has entrusted to us.
- In responding to the challenges of Christian stewardship in every area of life, we are called to shape decisions about our personal finances in light of God's claim on our lives.
- Tithing can provide a biblical, practical, timely giving guideline for Christian disciples.

The American Baptist Churches in the U.S.A. has formulated some of these points in its Policy Statement Encouraging the Tithe (1992), a portion of which I reproduce here:

TITHING IS BIBLICAL. It is a clear teaching within Old Testament law. This teaching is not abolished in the New Testament, but enriched and transformed by grace. Tithing, in light of the gospel, becomes a privilege under grace rather than an obligation under law. Tithing may be seen as a minimum standard for Christians seeking a biblical base for financial stewardship.

TITHING IS PRACTICAL. It can provide an economic base for the whole ministry of Christ's church. If we accept the standard of the tithe, there will be an abundance, recognizing and celebrating the goodness of God, supporting the ministry, providing places of worship, and ministering in ways we have not dreamed of with the poor, homeless, and oppressed.

TITHING IS TIMELY. Its message is needed now. The spirit of the age is to "get." The spirit of the tithe is to "give." The end of money is not to make life easier or more luxurious. For the Christian, the end of money is "that God's will shall be done on earth as it is in heaven."

Tithing is a discipleship issue, not a fund-raising device. It has to do with our relationship to Jesus Christ. The question tithing raises is not "how much of the church's budget is my share," but rather, "how much of my income is God's share." We have a need to give, and the tithe is a guide in addressing that need.

Tithing is:

- a source of blessing in our relationship with God;
- symbolic in putting God first;
- an act of gratitude for and an expression of commitment to God's work;
- an important element in Christian discipleship;
- a help in reordering priorities, establishing God's rightful place in our lives;
- capable of extending the church's witness and service through ministries near and far;
- able to free us from being vulnerable to greed, and to develop in us a new spirit of generosity in all things.

How to Help Stewards Deal with the Issues of Money and Possessions

Every congregation has a major responsibility to assist its stewards in dealing with the issues of money and possessions in today's world. The major role to be played in this process belongs to each church's chief stewards. In the account offered in Genesis 41–45, we find Joseph as one model of a chief steward. He was responsible for the work and welfare of many stewards (servants). Clergy and elected lay leaders in Christ's church fall into the category of chief stewards. To them much is given; of them much will be expected.

There are three arenas within which we traditionally deal with the issues of money and possessions: preaching, teaching, and modeling.

Preaching

Pastors need to address the contemporary issues of money and possessions from the pulpit, knowing full well that to preach as Christ did isn't necessarily going to win them many friends! They need to bring alive the biblical concepts of stewards, tithing, firstfruits, Jubilee restoration, loving, and sharing for today's Christians. We need to hear more sermons drawn from 2 Corinthians 8. Committed Christians will receive and take to heart such sermons if they are clearly grounded in Scripture and in love, even if they may be difficult to listen to.

Teaching

The biblical teaching concerning issues of wealth and appropriate applications to our current situation need to be presented to children, youth, and adults in every teaching arena available. Teaching can be even more effective than preaching in stimulating interest in and practical responses to such issues, since it more readily incorporates opportunities for dialogue, questioning, and debate. Each congregation faces a tremendous challenge to present biblical perspectives on money and possessions and to help children and youth respond as stewards.

Modeling

I believe the most effective method for encouraging stewardship is modeling. Jesus lived what he taught and preached. He didn't just talk about giving; he himself gave healing, comfort, instruction, hope, encouragement, vision, and even his life. He didn't just talk about forgiveness; on the cross, he prayed for the forgiveness of those who were persecuting him. The best way for us to help one another grow as stewards is to model all we have ourselves experienced about stewardship. Within the church, modeling begins with the clergy and lay leaders of the congregation — the chief stewards — but all of us are called to present authentic and vital models and to help one another meet our stewardship goals.

With these three arenas in mind, I would propose the following steps that Christian at the local church level might profitably take:

- Each congregation needs to determine who is responsible for making certain that biblical stewardship permeates the life of the church and its members.
- The subject of giving should be discussed openly by each congregation's membership rather than treated as a secret.
- Each congregation should establish tithing as a minimum goal toward which its members should strive — or move beyond. To this end, churches need to encourage practical standards for giving, both on a congregational level and on a personal level. "Serendipity giving," or "giving as the spirit moves," is inconsistent and undependable, motivated as it is solely by feelings of the moment. God expects more of us than that, and we should exhort one another to a better standard.
- Each congregation can encourage, support, and provide resources for every family unit in which there are children and young people and enable parents to talk about, teach, and model Christian stewardship in every aspect of life, including money.
- Each congregation should draw up a plan containing challenges to increase giving and expand its mission.
- Each congregation needs to determine the balance between how much it needs for its own ministry and how much it should share to extend the work of the larger church.
- Each congregation needs to examine its own internal procedures for receiving offerings to ensure that it is not providing poor models of what Christ-like giving is all about. For instance, if a congregation reduces its mission giving when local expenses rise, it may be sending the message to members that they should reduce their giving to the church the next time household expenses rise.
- Just as congregations need to focus special sorts of attention on encouraging children and young people to develop good attitudes toward giving, so they need to encourage their elderly members to explore ways in which they can continue to be good stewards of money, possessions, and resources in their changing circumstances. For most people, retirement entails a reduction in income but an increase in free time — and such changes should be reflected in their stewardship. They might also benefit

from seminars in estate planning and the like, to find ways to continue to support the work of God's church after death.

- Finally, in all our efforts to determine how much we should give, prayer should be an essential element. Congregations should pray urgently about money issues, and members should be educated in the importance of prayer in this regard. Let's face it: God doesn't have to wait for your money or mine. God is the "owner" of all the resources in the universe and is not limited by what we give. But we are partners with God. We're in this thing called life together! God rejoices when one of us takes another step in sharing money, resources, and possessions. It's one significant way in which we act to enter into partnership with God. Jesus gave of himself totally, "and a voice from heaven said, 'This is my Son, the Beloved, in whom I am well pleased.'" When Christ's followers live and give as Christian stewards, God also rejoices.

It's risky to pray about giving. You may end up giving more than you first intended! But what's wrong with that? It's a natural part of growing as one of God's stewards. My wife and I recently faced the challenge of giving the largest gift to God's work we had ever considered. We didn't know whether we could afford to do it. So we prayed over an extended period of time. Eventually our fears about the commitment were set aside, mostly by the quiet assurance that God will provide. After about ten months of prayer, we made the commitment. In the time since, we have found that God has in fact provided for us! Pray, and trust God to help you with the answers.

The question remains: "How much should I give?" Do you have a good idea of how much you are already giving? Many people don't have a very good handle on where their money goes. Take some time to go over whatever records you may have — old tax forms, bank statements, checkbook registers — and try to come up with some rough approximations of the sorts of things you're spending your money on. Use the pie chart on p. 67 as a guide and fill in dollar amounts and percentages. You can use whatever time period you feel is most appropriate, going back a few weeks, a few months, a year.

When you've finished, look to see if any of the numbers surprise you. Most of us have some general sense of what our priorities are, even if we haven't given it a lot of thought. How do you think that sense of priorities squares with the figures you have recorded in the chart? If someone who didn't know you looked at the figures, do you think that person might imagine that you have a different set of priorities? Can you see areas in which you wish the percentages were different? If so, can you think of any specific ways to change the configuration?

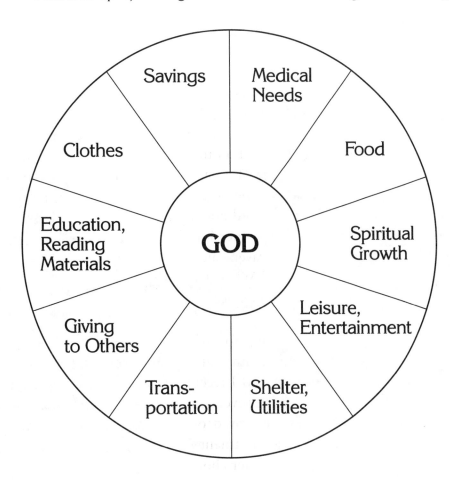

By way of conclusion, I want to leave this chapter somewhat open-ended. No one should tell you how much you should give. That is a matter for you, the steward, to work out with your Creator/Master/loving God. But as we think of Christ's commendation of the widow who placed her full week's salary in the offering plate, most of us probably feel the challenge to give more.

Perhaps we would do well to approach the question of how much we should give by asking ourselves how much we need to live comfortably. Instead of asking "How much should I give?" try asking "How much should I keep?" Instead of asking "What do I need that I don't have?" try asking "What do I have that I don't need?"

Obviously there is much more to be said about money, possessions, and tithing. But perhaps we have covered enough ground to set you thinking in new ways about your stewardship of this part of the wealth you have received. May God bless your efforts to be the best steward you can be of the resources with which you have been entrusted.

QUESTIONS FOR DISCUSSION

1. The Bible tells us that on more than one occasion, Jesus commended extravagant gifts — as in the case of the widow who gave a week's salary away without any apparent reserves, and the woman who gave him the gift of perfume worth a year's salary against the objections of the disciples, who said that the money might better have been used to provide food for the poor. Should we view gifts like these as rare exceptions to a standard of thoughtful stewardship, or do they constitute a wholly different standard? Have you ever felt that God was calling you to take a risk of this magnitude with your resources? If so, how did you respond?

2. Have you ever encountered an individual who wanted to give more than you felt was reasonable? Is it possible to be irresponsible in giving too much as well as in giving too little?

3. In the course of this chapter, we read Jesus' command in Matthew 5:42 — "Give to everyone who begs from you, and do not refuse anyone who wants to borrow from you." How do you think this applies in our culture? How do you respond when you are approached by people in the streets asking for money?

4. How much does your church give for ministries beyond your congregation compared with what it spends internally? Do you think that figure is appropriate, too high, or too low? Why?

5. Have you ever shared with anyone else how much you give away? If so, was the confidence returned, and what effect did the exchange have on you? If not, can you explain why you haven't done so?

6. Stewardship of God's Planet Earth

"In the beginning when God created the heavens and the earth . . ."

GENESIS 1:1

One Left Sneaker, Seven Drunken Snails!

Climbing Beaver Hill is my favorite physical exercise. Located a few hundred yards from our home, it offers a steep climb that tests the legs and lungs. I find it relaxing. The whole hike takes about forty-five minutes. To get to the hill, I walk on a paved road for a short distance, go through a covered bridge over French Creek, and then move into the woods. I often see deer and squirrels and on occasion have seen rabbits, woodchucks, turkey, possum, and, in the spring, trout in the creek.

I am also care-manager for this part of God's Planet Earth. There isn't any sign along the road telling you that. I just do it. Before I set out for a trip up the hill, I put a bag in my pocket, and along the way I pick up bottles and cans, plastic and junk. This is part of my steward's journey. Everything goes home into my garage or basement and is sorted for recycling. It seems there are some very careless stewards who travel the Beaver Hill Road — there is always something to pick up.

On a recent trip, I came home with one left sneaker and five aluminum cans. It was quite a find. If you know anyone who needs a left sneaker, size 9, I've got it. That would be recycling at its best! But the snails are another thing.

Snails love to crawl into discarded beer and soda cans. Apparently they like the remaining dregs in each. It's good stewardship to get the snails out of the can before taking them home. If you don't, eventually they smell — terrible! That's not pleasant for either me or the snails. So I set them free by shaking them out of each can along the way.

What a sight! They come out of the can in a dazed (drunken?) condition. They can't get their bearings. Once they are righted, they don't know which way to go and often just go in circles. How does a snail get rid of a hangover? Slowly, I guess, just like humans!

Beaver Hill is one small part of my world. Doubtless you have some treasured spots as well. All of us live out our lives on small patches of God's Planet Earth, which is itself one infinitesimally small patch of green and blue in the midst of a rapidly expanding universe. It boggles the mind to think about astronomical distances, about giant black holes and the countless galaxies flying away from one another in the dark reaches of space. For all its smallness and relative fragility in a universe that is by turn cold and explosive and generally hostile, however, we tend to take the earth for granted. We are so much smaller than the world we live on that nothing much we do seems to make a lasting difference to the ocean of air above us or the rocks and soil beneath our feet.

Next time you get the chance, though, pick up a bit of soil and squeeze it in your hand. Ask yourself where it came from. Ask yourself who owns it. Right now, let's look into what the Bible has to say about such matters.

What Do You Believe about God?

Over the centuries and today, there have been and are many images of God. Some are listed below. Place an "X" beside those that are connected with your understanding of God.

____ friend	____ distant
____ loving parent	____ untouchable
____ judge	____ all-knowing
____ creator	____ always accessible
____ boss	____ good
____ benevolent	____ touchable
____ absolute authority	____ angry

___ holy   ___ king

___ benefactor   ___ caring

___ sustainer of the universe   ___ manipulative

___ cop   ___ political

___ owner of the universe   ___ wholly other

___ warrior   ___ dispassionate

___ spirit   ___ unreachable

___ open   ___ righteous

You probably checked off many of the above. Compare the items you checked with those that others checked and see if you can account for any differences between your lists. Take another look at the list and underline the items that you associate with God specifically in the role of guardian of the physical world. Again, compare notes with others and discuss any differences in your lists.

To move toward an understanding of our role as stewards of Planet Earth, I want to take a close look at the biblical teachings regarding two aspects of the divine character: God as creator and God as owner of our world.

God the Creator

Both the Old and the New Testaments testify that God is the creator of all things. Indeed, the very first verse of the Bible states that "God created the heavens and the earth." God's act of creation is the starting point for our understanding of God, the world in which we live, ourselves, and the relationships of each to the others. And, having created all that there is, God continues to sustain it all moment by moment. Expressed throughout Scripture in story, song, hope, and formal statements of belief, the theme is the same: the triune God was, is, and will continue to be involved in all of creation.

In Genesis 1:2, we read of the divine involvement in the created order as "a wind from God" sweeping over the face of the waters. In John 1:3-4 we read that "all things came into being through him [Christ], and without him not one thing came into being. What has come into being in him was life, and the life was the light of all people." The one God — Parent, Son, and Holy Spirit — is Creator of all of nature.

The Bible portrays our creator God as both personal and spiritual, as not only bringing into being all that is but also sustaining it. Scripture teaches us that God's creation is good, even as God is good (Ps. 25:8; 34:8; Mark 10:18).

For some additional perspectives on God as Creator, see the following passages: Hebrews 11:3; Nehemiah 9:6; Deuteronomy 4:32; Psalm 8:3-8; 36:6; 148:1-12; Job 26:7; Isaiah 40:28; 45:5-8, 12, 18; Acts 14:15; Ephesians 2:10; 3:8-9; Colossians 1:15-17.

God the Owner

Christians believe that God created the universe and continues to sustain it, but many of them don't go beyond that in their thinking. They do not relate to the idea that God is owner of all that has been created. The cry "It is mine" has echoed through Western culture since the earliest days of the Roman Empire, changing little through the centuries. But thousands of years ago, God instructed the Israelites, "The land shall not be sold in perpetuity, for the land is mine; with me you are but aliens and tenants" (Lev. 25:23).

Jesus' parable of the absentee landlord (Matt. 21:33-41) tells of servants who misuse land entrusted to them and then go so far as to kill the son of the owner in their attempt to gain ownership. In his book *Stepping Stones of the Steward* Ronald E. Vallet says,

> "Turf protection" does not end as humans leave the family setting. . . . In the work setting, for example, you may be upset if someone who is not authorized to do so enters your office or opens a desk drawer. If another employee or department takes on a responsibility that you feel belongs to you or to your department, tension begins to build. . . . Such feelings of "turf protection" can erect barriers. . . .
>
> In other settings, "turf protection" creates bureaucratic "red tape," causing delays, inefficiencies, and injustices in institutions, business, industry, and government. Nations protect their turf, and wars result.
>
> In the parable of the absentee landlord, Jesus described a magnificent vineyard that belonged to a landowner who had left the vineyard to be worked by tenants and had gone into another country. The tenants were accountable for the fruits of the vineyard. Soon, however, the tenants began to think of the vineyard as belonging to them. Then the owner sent his son, thinking "They will respect my son" (Matt. 21:27). But they killed the son also.
>
> Of course, you are shocked when you hear such a story. But is it possible that humans are behaving similarly when we treat the planet Earth as "our vineyard" — to do as we wish with the fruits and even the vineyard itself? Do we forget that "The earth is the Lord's"? (Pp. 132-33)

Planet Earth is God's, not ours to do with as we please. More and more of the world's inhabitants are beginning to see implications of undisciplined exploitation of the earth's resources. There is an emerging concern worldwide that we need to become better care-managers of God's Planet Earth. Christians need to recognize daily the fact that "The earth is the Lord's."

The Creator/Owner God

There is a natural relationship between the concepts of divine creation and ownership. The concept of the Creator/Owner God is rich and powerful, and yet it is something we downplay or ignore in countless ways in our day-to-day life in a consumer culture. One of our greatest challenges as people of God is to bring ourselves and others face to face with the fact that God is the sole owner of all of creation. This sounds simple enough — what Christian would not consent to the assertion immediately? — and yet we often behave as though it had no practical implications for us. In fact, like many of God's truths, properly understood, it changes everything about how we view life. We need to confront this truth, and we need to confront our children with it. Perhaps if they are led to grapple with Jesus' model of ownership when they are young, they will be empowered to break free from the considerable power of the world's models and grow up to adopt a genuinely different treatment of life and the earth's resources.

Time and Creation

If you do take the opportunity to hold some soil in your hands, you will be grasping something that is literally millions of years old. Such expanses of time tend to be quite foreign to those who live in a consumer society. Our insatiable desire for instant gratification dims our ability to understand our environment in any depth, constructed as it is by processes drenched with antiquity, processes that tower above us and our frantic schedules. We sail down interstates beside mountain ranges pushed up hundreds of millions of years ago and worry about whether we'll get to the soccer match on time. On the way out the door, we grab a glass of water that has been cycling from the ocean to the rain clouds to groundwater aquifers for untold epochs, and our thoughts are on whether we'll make it to the store before it closes. On vacation, we sit on the rim of the Grand Canyon, carved out of solid rock by nothing more than running water over untold eons, and we wolf down fast food, planning the next stop. For the most part, we go through life oblivious to the depths of time all around us.

We don't pay all that much attention to the future either. There is an Amish proverb that echoes a Native American saying to the effect that we don't inherit the world from our ancestors; we borrow it from our children. In their simple approach to life, the Amish have a profound understanding of our relationship to the soil — and the implications of that relationship for the legacy we leave to those who follow us.

The U.S. National Parks Service has published "disintegration" guidelines meant to serve as something of a wake-up call for our throwaway society. As you head for the trash container, it might be helpful to think of the disintegration time for some everyday items you use:

Paper	2-5 months
Orange peels	6 months
Cotton rags	1-5 months
Rope	3-14 months
Milk carton	5 years
Filter tip cigarettes	1-12 years
Plastic bags	10-20 years
Leather shoes	25-40 years
Nylon cloth	30-40 years
Plastic containers	50-80 years
Soup cans	100 years
Aluminum	200-500 years
Plastic rings	450-? years
Styrofoam	never

We are a society of instant coffee, microwave ovens, fast food, fast everything. Sue Shaw, writing for the 1990 Church World Service Global Calendar, offered the following timely thoughts about fast-food hamburgers:

Here comes the succulent hamburger dripping with ketchup. Fast food for speedy times. The young woman perches uncomfortably on her hard plastic stool; eat up; hurry out. Stay no longer than you need. She unwraps the burger, takes her first bite. The packaging falls to the floor in her haste; bus to catch, no time to waste.

The woman watches herself eating in the wall mirror opposite. She has no idea where the beef she chews comes from; no time to ask. It might stick in her throat if she knew.

The international beef industry is always seeking out cheaper meat and some places produce cattle at less cost than others. "It boils down to $95 per cow per year in Montana, $25 in Costa Rica," says one rancher. The cheaper the cows, the bigger the business. So rain forests are felled, land is cleared, grass planted, cheap beef is produced, and consumer demand is satisfied. The pasture doesn't last long, however, because the soil is quickly leached of its nutrients and left barren from over-grazing. In a few years it becomes useless and the whole process begins again somewhere else.

The woman takes her third bite and looks inside her bag. Perhaps she is wondering about the cost of her snack. Whatever her guess, she would be wrong. For the tropical forest they destroyed to make it took maybe 180 million years to grow. Rare animal species were wiped off the face of the earth forever. And indigenous people were hounded from their homes — even murdered — so that ranchers could take their land. A hectare of rain forest supports about 800,000 kilograms of plants and animals. The same hectare cleared for cattle grazing will produce at most 200 kilograms of meat a year — enough for just 1,600 hamburgers.

Our friend pops the final lump of burger into her mouth. She looks at her fingers, satiated, unaware that her meal has contributed to someone else's hunger. The populations who live where trees once grew have no animals left to hunt, nor any fertile land on which to grow crops. And the earth, laid bare to the elements, turns to desert. In Ethiopia, for example, the forests that once clothed the land have practically disappeared while famine is almost an annual event; and still Ethiopian beef is exported to the West.

Four bites and the hamburger is finished. Fast food. The bus pulls up outside, and the woman leaves. Perhaps it is the jolting of the vehicle that makes her feel queasy, or the result of her mad rush. It could be the hamburger itself, cocktail of fat, flavorings, and colorants swirling around inside. Or maybe indigestion is inevitable, after eating half a ton of tropical rain forest.

What Are We Doing to God's Planet Earth?

Just as our choices as individuals about such matters as where we choose to have dinner have wide-ranging implications with respect to stewardship, so the choices that we make corporately are important. Indeed, the sorts of choices that the nations of the world have made to defend themselves in this century have affected the shape of life on God's Planet Earth almost incalculably. And it's not only the bombs that have been dropped and the bullets that have been fired that have rewritten our history: the stockpiles of weapons and armaments that sit unused also constitute an enormous weight of threat and missed potential.

Over forty years ago, President Dwight D. Eisenhower spoke words that remain fully relevant today:

Every gun that is made, every warship launched, every rocket fired signifies, in the final sense, a theft from those who hunger and are not fed, those who are cold and not clothed.

This world in arms is not spending money alone.

It is spending the seat of its laborers, the genius of its scientists, the hopes of its children.

The cost of one modern heavy bomber is this: a modern brick school in more than 30 cities.

It is two electric power plants, each serving a town of 60,000 population. It is two fine, fully equipped hospitals. It is some 50 miles of concrete highway.

We pay for a single fighter plane with a half million bushels of wheat. We pay for a single destroyer with new homes that could have housed more than 8,000 people.

This, I repeat, is the best way of life to be found on the road the world has been taking.

This is not a way of life at all, in any true sense. Under the cloud of threatening war, it is humanity hanging from a cross of iron.

How can you become a better steward of God's Planet Earth?

Think for a moment about your community. In the left column of the list below, put down some things that you feel are not currently being adequately care-managed by anyone. In the right column, list some things that are being appropriately care-managed. Place a star next to the items in the right column if the care-managing is being done by people from the church.

Not Being Care-Managed   **Are Being Care-Managed**

_____   _____

_____   _____

_____   _____

_____   _____

_____   _____

_____   _____

_____   _____

Where is the Church in the Struggle to Save God's Planet Earth?

I have suggested that the first step of stewardship is the act of entrusting. Early in the biblical account, God turned over to humans the earth and all that is on it. God entrusted the soil, water, and air into our hands, and we've been in charge ever since. Christians have received a special trust in the sense that we have been named joint heirs with Christ by the Owner.

The evidence is mounting that we who profess to be in alliance with God have been less than effective advocates of God's creation. Can we expect the fields of science or engineering to make up for our shortcomings as stewards? Two men, one a chemist and the other an anthropologist, recently stated that they saw no hope for Planet Earth coming from the disciplines to which they had devoted their lives. If we are to find answers to our environmental plight, they will have to come first of all not from the realm of science but from the realm of love, the realm of the spiritual. "Don't look to the Republicans, Democrats, Exxon Oil Company, or anyone else to change the human heart," they said. "That can come only through the church."

This is our challenge: responding as the church of Jesus Christ to the challenge of being good care-managers of God's Planet Earth. What can we as individual stewards do to make a difference? Consider the following:

1. Read the Scriptures with an eye to learning more about what God has created and your personal role as a care-manager of what God has created.
2. Make the term "God's Planet Earth" a familiar part of your vocabulary. This phrase is testimony to anyone listening that you believe God is the Creator/Owner. This needs to be declared from the mountaintops! Pastors can use the term in sermons, Sunday school teachers in their classes, parents with their children. Rename Earth Day "God's Planet Earth Day."

3. Choose a specific piece of God's Planet Earth to care-manage. The sheer size of the earth and of the environmental problems we face makes many think that there's nothing one person can do to change things. That simply isn't true. Even if you live in the deepest inner-city in North America, you can find some little patch of ground somewhere that can be improved with your care. Be responsible. Pick out a piece of God's Planet Earth and put your name on it. Then take care of it — however you decide to do so.

4. Act on the belief that one person can make a difference. I began a crusade against the use of styrofoam cups awhile back and was pleasantly surprised when my home church joined in the crusade with me. Similar efforts elsewhere are likewise meeting with success, and styrofoam cups are beginning to disappear from our homes, schools, and places of business. Quite some time ago, a Girl Scout troop of First Baptist Church in Kittanning, Pennsylvania, petitioned McDonald's to stop using styrofoam containers. Despite meeting with initial resistance and discouragement, they kept up their campaign, and, in concert with many others, they eventually convinced the fast-food giant to make a change. One person, one group, one congregation *can* make a difference. Don't underestimate what you can do!

5. Make an effort to pass what you have learned along to members of your family. Naturally, parents should serve as models of stewardship for their children, but children can also inform and encourage adult members of the family. The family is often the most influential setting in which stewardship habits are developed.

6. Believe in and practice recycling. All manner of materials — paper, cardboard, aluminum, glass, metal, plastic — can be recycled. It takes time and a bit of effort, but it is very important. I do not have curbside recycling in my community, so I have to collect material until I have a carful to take to a recycling center. My garage and basement usually contain a few boxes and bags of the cans and bottles I've picked up along the roadside as I do my exercise walk up Beaver Hill Road. It is often dirty and time-consuming work, but I have taken it as my personal responsibility to care-manage this bit of God's Planet Earth. I encourage you to be diligent about recycling, too, not only in and around your home but in your school or workplace as well.

7. Subscribe to a paper or magazine that informs and enlightens you on current events regarding stewardship and God's Planet Earth. There are a number of these. One is *Food and Hunger Notes* (21 South 12th Street, P.O. Box 500, Akron, Pennsylvania 17501-0500), a very informative paper

produced by the Mennonite Central Committee. Perhaps you could establish a subscription for your church.

8. Learn about the ways in which all parts of God's creations are interrelated and how it is impossible to harm one part of creation without harming other parts. Genesis 1 presents the picture of a unity of creation: all parts interrelated, and all together belonging to God. Even mosquitoes and rattlesnakes have important parts to play in God's overall design.

9. Begin to change your lifestyle. Find ways to decrease your use of nonrenewable resources. If you need to own a car, get one with good gas mileage, and try to use it less. Walk short distances; use a bicycle if you're able; consolidate trips. Changes don't have to be elaborate to be effective!

10. Become a partner with God in advocating the preservation of God's Planet Earth. God needs a lot of partners today — there aren't many around. It doesn't take special training or a lot of money. Many books today provide new ideas about how to be such a partner with God.

11. Plant trees. Trees absorb greenhouse gases, prevent soil erosion, provide homes for birds and other animals, and enrich our lives with their beauty. Seedlings are available from a variety of government agencies and private groups such as scout troops. If you don't have any acreage of your own on which to plant, there are national and local programs in which your participation would be welcomed. For suggestions, contact the nearest office of the U.S. Forest Service.

12. Become a confronter! After you have educated yourself about the current state of affairs on God's Planet Earth, help bring someone else face to face with it. Teach your children, your grandchildren, your neighbor's children about the need to care for God's planet. Take the effort to make your home as energy efficient as it can be. Confront local, state, and national legislators with your concerns for God's Planet Earth, too. Be heard!

Make a list of ways in which your congregation is involved in stewardship of God's Planet Earth.

_____

_____

_____

_____

_____

_____

_____

_____

_____

_____

Can you think of any ways in which your congregation has been lax in its environmental stewardship? Are you willing to do something about it?

The Church as Care-Manager

Strength and wisdom are generated when Christians act together. This can be beneficial to the cause of caring for the world God has entrusted to our care. The following are some things you could do at the congregational level:

1. Encourage your pastor, Sunday school teachers, youth counselors, and other church educators to use the term "God's Planet Earth" and to work to underscore the significance of its meaning in the context of daily life.
2. Choose which piece of God's Planet Earth your congregation will care-manage. A natural choice would be the church grounds, but consider looking beyond that as well. Some communities have programs in which groups pledge to care for a given stretch of highway or do park maintenance, for example.
3. Establish a conversation with the neighborhood surrounding your church building and try to find ways to approach stewardship of your common resources together.
4. Monitor your recycling habits. Congregations should model recycling.
5. Ask your pastor to preach on biblical passages that point to God's Creator/Owner role. Other sermon subjects could include your congregation's corporate role as a care-manager as well as your roles as individual Christian stewards.
6. Obtain and advertise literature, videotapes, and the like that present issues and opportunities associated with the care of God's Planet Earth.
7. Emphasize the interrelatedness of God's whole creation. Look into the

sources of all the goods and services your church buys and uses and see if you can't find better alternatives.

8. Help your congregation decrease its demand for nonrenewable sources of energy. Is your building as energy efficient as it can be? Arrange with your local utilities for an audit of your congregation's energy use and then implement any recommended changes.

9. Ask whether your church needs to make some lifestyle changes such as giving up the convenience of disposable plates and cups or dialing back the thermostat. Look for ways in which you can make a personal sacrifice or contribution.

10. Ask your church to pledge itself to intentional, active partnership with God in caring for our earth.

11. Sponsor the planting of at least one tree a year. Encourage a youth group to adopt part of a nearby stream or body of water, monitor the level of pollution in it, and work to clean up its shoreline at regular intervals.

12. Encourage members of your congregation to walk or carpool to services. Each gallon of gas burned adds nineteen pounds of carbon dioxide to the atmosphere.

13. Bring specific legislative initiatives to your congregation's attention and encourage members to write to local, state, and federal representatives about your concerns for the care of God's Planet Earth.

14. Create small study groups to focus on some of the issues that God's Planet Earth is facing.

15. Invite speakers to address your church, Sunday school, youth, and other groups about issues of environmental stewardship.

16. Use recycled paper for your congregation's printing jobs.

17. Pray as individuals and as a congregation for God's wisdom and empowerment in all your efforts to address the challenges of care-managing God's Planet Earth.

18. Become a confronter as a congregation! Ask your church to bring your own members, your own community — yes, even the world — face to face with the fact that we are stewards of God's creation.

Summary

Mennonites tell of the days when "soil evangelists" used to make the rounds of churches and farmers' gatherings to ask for commitments from the farmers to save the soil for future generations in obedience to God. As one Mennonite leader, Melvin D. Schmidt, put it in the pages of the November 1988 issue of *Builder* magazine,

> If we are really serious about the spiritual dimensions of the ecological crisis, we know that we will need to do more than just talk about enlightened self-interest. We will need to talk about the purposes for which God created us and our world. Did God actually bring this beautiful world into being so that it could be destroyed in less than five hundred years of modern agriculture and industry? In the Bible we see total redemption of the earth as God's plan — not total destruction. The total destruction is always the judgment that comes when sinning against the earth has taken place.
>
> In other words, our vision of salvation will have to be recast in more than just personal terms. I encountered this reality in a new way last spring, when it seemed that those good old gospel hymns speak of total salvation, not just personal salvation.
>
> I did not expect to find it in that old favorite gospel song remembered from my youth, but there it is: "Waft it on the rolling tide, Jesus Saves! Jesus Saves! Tell to sinners far and wide, Jesus Saves! Jesus Saves! Sing, ye islands of the sea, echo back, ye ocean caves! Earth shall keep her jubilee: Jesus Saves! Jesus Saves!"
>
> Can we sing "Jesus Saves" in the light of the disastrous oil spills? Or medical waste on the beaches? Does Jesus save the rolling tides and the islands of the sea? Can the earth keep her jubilee and sing for joy while covered with sludge and waste?

What will you, as one of God's care-managers, do with God's Planet Earth?

QUESTIONS FOR DISCUSSION

1. Our nation has experienced an ongoing debate in which the need to preserve the natural environment has been pitted against the need to preserve jobs. One example is the situation in the Pacific Northwest, where efforts to protect the habitat of species such as the Northern Spotted Owl have limited logging and put people out of work. How would you defend your point of view on this issue to someone who held the opposite point of view? In formulating your argument, specifi-

cally address the issue of our obligation to be good care-managers of God's Planet Earth.

2. The effort to be better stewards of God's Planet Earth may well involve costs in certain areas — time, convenience, money. How willing are you to accept such costs on a day-to-day basis? Do you accept the inconvenience of carpooling, for example? The discomfort of a lower thermostat setting during the winter months or reduced air conditioning during the summer? The greater expense of products made of recycled materials? Would you accept a smaller paycheck if your employer used the difference to pay for anti-pollution devices? Would you argue that people closer to the poverty line should make such sacrifices?

3. Can you see ways in which you might be able to be more effective in accomplishing your work of stewardship through cooperation with such "secular" environmental organizations as Friends of the Earth, the Sierra Club, and Greenpeace? Can you think of any ways in which a specifically Christian witness might conflict with the goals or approaches of such organizations?

4. What resources has your congregation devoted to the stewardship of what God has entrusted to you? Have you budgeted any money specifically to care for God's Planet Earth? If so, do you believe the figure is appropriate? If not, evaluate your reasons for deciding not to do so.

5. Years ago, ranchers in the American West sought to protect their cattle by eradicating predators such as mountain lions, coyotes, and wolves. They were especially effective in driving the wolf population out of huge areas of range land. Recently, a controversy has arisen over attempts to return wolves to what was once their natural habitat. How does your understanding of God's creation inform your perspective on this controversy? Does the interrelatedness of all parts of the creation mean that attempts to control or eliminate predators are wrong? If you were a rancher, what stand would you take on the proposal to return wolves to your area? Are there any "pests" that you feel justified in trying to eliminate?

7. Stewardship of God's Gifts of Life and Time

"Finally, beloved, whatever is true, whatever is honorable, whatever is just, whatever is pure, whatever is pleasing, whatever is commendable, if there is any excellence and if there is anything worthy of praise, think about these things."

PHILIPPIANS 4:8

The place was Romania in the 1960s. Their names were Peter and Florica. He was thirty and she was twenty-eight. They were committed followers of Christ who believed strongly in God's presence in their lives. They were the parents of two wonderful boys, aged four and five. Florica had had a very difficult birth experience with the second boy, however, and their doctor had warned that Florica should never have another child.

Several years later, Florica suspected that she was pregnant. She shared her concern with Peter. They waited and prayed for God's guidance. After three months, she went to her doctor. The doctor told her that if she tried to bring the child to term, it would kill her, and he advised an immediate abortion. She and Peter spent many weeks praying to know God's will in their lives and that of the unborn child. In the end, Florica said, "This child is a gift from God. I must care for God's gift. If I die in order for this gift to live, so be it."

The months were fulfilled and the baby was born. Within eight hours of

84

the birth, Florica died. Before death, she named her child Benoni, but Peter called him Benjamin (see Gen. 35:16-20). Benoni Benjamin, now a young and energetic pastor in Romania, told me this story with tears in his eyes. Life for him had meant death for another. It was, indeed, a costly gift. Only because his mother chose life for him is he alive today. He is a young leader among Baptists in Romania and praises God for the gift of life from his mother and from his God. He is strongly committed to inviting others to experience new life through Christ, who died that they might live.

Florica could have reacted in several different ways. Whether we agree or disagree with the course of action that she and Peter chose is not the point of the story. The important point is not *what* their decision was but that their decision emerged from intense consultation with their God, the giver of life. They recognized God as the author of life and, after months of intense prayer, responded as they felt God wanted them to respond. The Creator/Owner/Sustainer God desires that all Christians make their life-and-death decisions in a similar manner. How much is a life worth? How do we place a value on living or dying? Few of us have had to face a situation like Peter and Florica's, but if you were faced with circumstances of similar gravity tomorrow, how would you make your decision?

Scripture clearly teaches that life is a gift from God. Genesis 2:7 states that "the Lord God formed us of dust from the ground, and breathed into our nostrils the breath of life; and we became living beings" (my translation). God entrusts a certain number of years to each of us, gives us a road to travel and a vision to guide us. Then God turns us loose to care-manage the life entrusted to us. It is not ours to keep, even if we try to do so.

Questions such as "Where did I come from?" "Where am I going?" and "How much time have I been allotted?" usually point to a person's search for life's meaning. Some begin to ask such questions early in life. Others begin to ponder them later, often in the midst of traumatic or unsettling life events. Some people never get around to dealing with life questions at all. Recognizing that there may be a purpose to life that provides answers to life's Why questions can move us to explore the gift of life itself.

The Richness of the Gift of Life

Jesus asked, "What will it profit them if they gain the whole world but forfeit their life? Or what will they give in return for their life?" (Matt. 16:26). He was saying that nothing else can compare with the value of life itself. Christians, especially, know this is true, since we believe our spiritual journey will last far beyond our physical journey. We have been entrusted with the assurance that death does not end the gift of life but is the door to life everlasting. John recorded the assurance that Jesus gave his disciples — and us — as the trial of the crucifixion neared: "In my Father's house there are many dwelling places. If it were not so, would I have told you that I go to prepare a place for you? And if I go and prepare a place for you, I will come again and will take you to myself, so that where I am, there you may be also" (John 14:2-3).

The rich gift of life has many aspects. We come into the world as babies — physically, mentally, and spiritually. One of life's most fulfilling dimensions is our capacity to grow. Watching a baby grow is a beautiful experience, too. We marvel over the first word, first crawl, first step. Life is at its best when growth is taking place — no matter how old we are. When physical growth slows later in life, we still marvel at the possibilities of continuing to grow mentally, spiritually, and relationally. Since the scope of stewardship covers all aspects of life, we have all manner of opportunities to grow as stewards.

The process of growth intimately connects past, present, and future. Life presents us with certain categories of experience again and again. If we are properly aware and prepared, we can respond to these circumstances in ways that are increasingly meaningful and profound. And the Bible informs us that we have an obligation to make something of our life journey, to redeem the time we are given, to grow in the ways of the Lord. Again I cite Paul's confession in this regard: "When I was a child, I spoke like a child, I thought like a child, I reasoned like a child; when I became an adult, I put an end to childish ways" (1 Cor. 13:11). Paul recognized that the heart of the faith journey is the ability to grow. From beginning to end, our lives — physical, mental, and spiritual — are treasures entrusted to us by God. They are ours to care-manage.

The Gift of Physical Life

The gift of life has a very real physical dimension. God has made us physical creatures, and our bodies shape and define how we perceive the world, how we pass through it. The human body is stunningly complex. Even the simplest of its mechanical systems is awe-inspiring, and much of it continues to defy all understanding despite our meticulous and subtle analysis. When our bodies are working right physically, we are capable of extraordinary things; when they don't work right in even small ways, we are quickly brought face to face with our creaturely limitations.

A good care-manager pays attention to the gift of physical life. Many of us have learned the hard lesson of what can happen when our bodies are abused. We tend to act as though our bodies are capable of anything and have no limits. When a young movie star was recently warned that the volume at which he listened to his car stereo was damaging his hearing, his response was, "I'm stupid, I know that. But I'm not going to worry about the future." That attitude is unfortunately pervasive. Any reasonably educated person in our society knows that smoking, a poor diet, drinking to excess, long-term exposure to the sun, unsafe sex habits, and the like all present very real and very possibly fatal dangers, and yet how many of us continue to harbor our little vices regardless? Our bodies cannot and will not accept extended abuse. The call to stewardship includes a call to good care-managing of our bodies.

List some things you are currently doing that you feel exhibit good care-managing of your body.

_____

_____

_____

_____

_____

_____

_____

_____

_____

If you have ever been told by a doctor, spouse, friend, newspaper article, or the like that you should change some aspect of the way you care for your body, list that here.

_____

_____

_____

_____

_____

_____

_____

_____

_____

_____

Did you follow the advice? What were your reasons for accepting or rejecting it?

God's Gift of the Mind

Another dimension of the gift of life is our mind, our ability to think, analyze, plan. Being made in the image of God suggests that we can think, reason, and plan in a manner similar to the Creator God. Care of the mind is as important as care of the body. As we tend to discover sooner or later, the two are connected in important ways: a healthy mind has much to do with a healthy body. The reverse is just as true.

The Bible suggests that it is wise and good to be thoughtful. The Psalmist wrote, "When I think of your ways, I turn my feet to your decrees" (119:59). As the passage from Philippians cited at the head of this chapter indicates, Paul recommends our reflection on all that is pure, pleasing, commendable, excellent, and worthy of praise.

In our culture, we tend to be less careful about maintaining the health of the mind than we are about maintaining the health of the body. We know we should floss and brush our teeth regularly, but how many of us make an effort to freshen our thinking ability on a daily basis? It need not be difficult, though it will call for a little self-discipline. It can be as simple as switching off the television and picking up a challenging book instead — or setting the book aside to have a conversation with someone else. Discussing almost any subject will tend to get you to think about it more clearly. Small groups, whether formal or informal, can also provide a stimulating context for thought and reflection. And many marriages would be more stable if the partners regularly talked with one another about something more significant than the dinner menu or who was going to take out the trash.

List three things you do on a regular basis to improve your mind. If you can't think of three things, fill out the list with things you will make an effort to do in the future.

1. _____

_____

2. _____

_____

3. _____

_____

God's Gift of Spiritual Life

Most people in our culture pay even less attention to their spiritual health than they do to their physical or mental health, and yet as Christians we must make our spiritual well-being a top priority. Paul left no question about the importance he attached to his spiritual side when he said, "To me, living is Christ and dying is gain" (Phil. 1:21). In Deuteronomy we read that "one does not live by bread alone, but by every word that comes from the mouth of the LORD" (8:3). In the Gospel of John we read Jesus' words on the issue: "Very truly I tell you, anyone who hears my word and believes him who sent me has eternal life, and does not come under judgment, but has passed from death to life" (5:24) and "Very truly, I tell you, no one can see the kingdom of God without being born from above" (3:3). The biblical metaphor of the journey of faith points to our potential and need for spiritual growth. If the simple faith and prayers of our youth do not grow, blossom, and flower into the fullness of an adult expression of faith, then something is wrong.

Our spiritual side needs care-managing. Worship, whether inside or outside a church sanctuary, is vital for our spiritual health. God constantly calls us to a spiritual journey that is new, fresh, vital, and stimulating. When we respond to God's call, life can take on new meaning and dimensions. As we grow older, we tend to become more resistant to change, to long for the comfort of the familiar. But God, our source of vision and strength, can help us break through the human fear of change. We need not be afraid to seek God in new ways every day of our lives. I don't know how long I'll live, but it is my hope that right up to the moment I draw my last breath I'll be learning new things about God. The call to expand our awareness of the encompassing reality of God may well be life's greatest challenge, but it is also the most rewarding.

List some experiences, relationships, or events you feel are helpful to your spiritual growth.

_____

_____

_____

_____

_____

_____

_____

_____

_____

List three specific spiritual goals in your faith journey that you have yet to accomplish and place a check beside your highest priority.

1. _____

_____

2. _____

_____

3. _____

_____

Care-Managing Your Gift of Life from God

How are you doing with the gift of life that God has entrusted to you? Life is often so busy that many of us don't set aside as much time for personal self-assessment as we do to maintain our cars. Take some time now to look back over the lists you filled out under the headings of the physical, mental, and spiritual aspects of your life. First try to give a realistic assessment of your relative strengths and weaknesses in each of the three categories. Then compare the level of effort you give to care-managing the three categories relative to one another. Ask yourself questions like the following: Do you devote such long hours to sports or workouts at the health club that you have no time left to read or to devote to the important relationships in your life? Do you spend so much time reading, taking classes, attending seminars, watching films, and talking to friends and colleagues that you have no time left for prayer, worship, and Bible study? Does your involvement in spiritual concerns lead you to devalue the "things of the flesh," to dismiss exercise as unimportant, to be careless about diet and other physical health concerns?

In calling us to care-manage the gift of life, God calls us not only to stewardship of the physical, mental, and spiritual aspects of our lives but also to maintenance of an appropriate balance among the three. Continue your self-assessment in conversation with God. Talk about your gift of life, and be open to what God has to share with you on this subject.

The Richness of God's Gift of Time

Few among us seem satisfied with the pace of time. Kids and parents sail off in all directions frantically trying to meet individual schedules, some days talking to one another only during brief midflight pauses. For some elderly and bed-ridden people, on the other hand, the hours and days drag by only too slowly. Children can't wait to become teens, teens can't wait to become adults, and adults find that the years fly by at increasing speeds. Some of us can hardly catch our breath. Others of us find time hanging heavy on our hands. Only a lucky few of us manage to drain each day dry without feeling harried.

For most of us, time and life are fleeting. In 1 Chronicles 29:15 we read that "our days on the earth are like a shadow, and there is no hope." In the depths of despair, Job said, "My days are swifter than a weaver's shuttle, and come to the end without hope" (7:6). The Psalmist cried out, "You have made my days a few handbreadths, and my lifetime is as nothing in your sight" (39:5). See also Psalm 89:47; 90:9; 102:11; and Ecclesiastes 6:12.

Scripture also makes distinctions between time (the human realm) and eternity (the divine realm). For example, 2 Peter 3:8 suggests that "with the Lord one day is like a thousand years, and a thousand years are like one day" (cf. Ps. 90:4). The concept of eternal life after physical death — that is, life beyond the bounds of time — had great significance for Jesus and his followers. In John 3:14-15 we read that Jesus said, "The Son of Man [must] be lifted up, that whoever believes in him may have eternal life." He lived and died and rose to free us from the shackles of time, if we but believe.

One of the New Testament's most pointed statements about time appears in James 4:13-14: "Come now, you who say, 'Today or tomorrow we will go to such and such a town and spend a year there, doing business and making money.' Yet you do not even know what tomorrow will bring. What is your life? For you are a mist that appears for a little while and then vanishes." The richness of our days lies not in their length or number but in the fact that we have received them as a gift from God.

Our Place in Time

The concept of time is fascinating. Everything we think and do is bounded by time. We can't even imagine any sort of existence apart from time. The closest we can come to understanding eternity is to think of it as time without end, rather than the absence of time. But despite the fact that we live immersed in time like fish live immersed in water, we have little idea of what it really is. The more modern physicists work out the complex mathematics of the relationship between time and space and motion, the stranger it looks. Few of us can hope to plumb such depths, but on a quite different level, we *can* develop an understanding of time that will help us better care-manage the portion of it that God gives us.

We live poised on a moment, suspended between a rich and meaningful past and a future that is often uncertain in the near term but made ultimately secure by Christ's sacrifice for us. As we live our lives, we establish relationships to both past and future that can be either appropriate and healthful or inappropriate and destructive. The Bible offers us valuable guidelines for charting our way in these relationships.

- We must not cling to the past. "If anyone is in Christ, there is a new creation: everything old has passed away; see, everything has become new!" (2 Cor. 5:17).
- Neither must we ignore the past. "Remember the former things of old;

for I am God, and there is no other; I am God and there is no one like me, declaring the end from the beginning and from ancient times the things not yet done, saying, 'My purpose shall stand, and I will fulfill my intention'" (Isa. 46:9-10).

- We cannot find our way to the future without some judicious reflection on the past. If we do not learn from our mistakes, we will repeat them; if we do not come to terms with old wounds (both those we have received and those we have given), the pain we carry with us will blind us to new opportunities; if we do not remember God's grace to us in the past, we will not think to look for it in the future. It is true that we are called to put to death all that is evil in our past, but as we are raised to new life in Christ, this past is not simply discarded: it is renewed. We are renewed not to innocence of our past but to wisdom concerning it. "Put to death . . . whatever in you is earthly: fornication, impurity, passion, evil desire, and greed (which is idolatry). On account of these the wrath of God is coming on those who are disobedient. These are the ways you also once followed, when you were living that life. But now you must get rid of all such things — anger, wrath, malice, slander, and abusive language from your mouth. Do not lie to one another, seeing that you have stripped off the old self with its practices and have clothed yourself with the new self, which is being renewed in knowledge according to the image of its creator. In that renewal there is no longer Greek and Jew, circumcised and un-circumcised, barbarian, Scythian, slave and free; but Christ is all in all!" (Col. 3:5-11).

- As we look to the future, we must be not be overconfident of our own strength to determine our destinies. "And I will say to my soul, 'Soul, you have ample good laid up for many years; relax, eat, drink, be merry.' But God said to him, 'You fool! This very night your life is being demanded of you. And the things you have prepared, whose will they be?'" (Luke 12:19-20).

- Neither should we allow ourselves to be crippled by concerns for our future well-being. "I tell you, do not worry about your life, what you will eat or what you will drink, or about your body, what you will wear. Is not life more than food, and the body more than clothing? . . . And can any of you by worrying add a single hour to your span of life?" (Matt. 6:25, 27).

- On the other hand, neither should we be irresponsibly careless about the future. "Which of you, intending to build a tower, does not first sit down and estimate the cost, to see whether he has enough to complete it?" (Luke 14:28).

We live to some degree in the midst of uncertainty. We cannot know how the details of our lives will unfold, what nations will rise and fall, what joys and sorrows we will have to face individually. But in the midst of this uncertainty, the word of God serves as an anchor. "Heaven and earth will pass away, but my words will not pass away. But about that day or hour no one knows, neither the angels in heaven, nor the Son, but only the Father. Beware, keep alert; for you do not know when the time will come" (Mark 13:31-33). We do not know what tomorrow will bring, but we can be certain that the future — and, indeed, every moment — lies in the hand of God. Whatever our place in time, God holds us secure.

Christians Are Care-Managers of God's Gift of Time

Each Christian is a steward of God's gift of time. How do you use this gift from God? Most of us are familiar enough with the concept of tithing our income, but have you ever considered tithing your time? Given the hectic schedules that most people in our culture have, I suspect that most of us would rather pledge money than time. But does God expect us to make some of our limited time available for God's purposes?

Some people obviously think so. They're the ones who volunteer to teach a Sunday school class, who help transport people to doctors' offices, who visit shut-ins who have no family of their own, who devote their time to providing the thousand little expressions of love that sustain the body of Christ. It is a fact that in most congregations about 20 percent of the members provide about 80 percent of the leadership (time *and* money). We all know that Jesus said, "Where your treasure is, there your heart will be also" (Matt. 6:21; Luke 12:34), but we don't all find the time to demonstrate that we know it.

As you contemplate how you use twenty-four hours each day, how do you feel about your care-managing of time? Are you a good steward of God's gift of time? Does your life express a good balance between personal/private time and time given to others? Do you make time to commune with God on a regular basis? Most Christians acknowledge the importance of prayer, but when they are pressed for time, prayer is often one of the first things to be sacrificed. Some of us seem to wish there was a substitute for taking time to pray. But reading about prayer is not praying. Talking about prayer is not praying. Reflecting on prayer is not praying. There are no substitutes, and a healthy prayer life will place certain demands on your time. But time spent in prayer, unlike so many of our other pursuits, is never ill-spent. Prayer is our most energizing, supportive, encouraging use of time. When we pray, we are in direct contact with the Giver of the gift of time.

Although many Bible readers seem to think that Jesus was talking only about money in the discourse recorded in Matthew 6:19-21, he was talking about time as well: "Do not store up for yourselves treasures on earth, where moth and rust consume and where thieves break in and steal, but store up for yourselves treasures in heaven, where neither moth nor rust consumes and where thieves do not break in and steal. For where your treasure is, there your heart will be also." Indeed, God may well consider gifts of our time to be more valuable than gifts of our money. Which sort of gift would you rather receive from someone you love — a check or an evening? One practical way in which we can give God gifts of time is to give some of that time to others. "Truly I tell you, just as you did it to one of the least of these who are members of my family, you did it to me" (Matt. 25:40).

One significant fact emerges in every professional time management seminar: very few people actually know how they use their time. We all have rough ideas about how much time we spend on various parts of our lives, but our perceptions can be inaccurate. Some people perceive an hour spent in church to be a good deal longer than an hour spent in front of the television set, and, working from that sort of perception, they might be inclined to think they spend more time worshiping than amusing themselves in an average week even if the opposite is true.

Before we can take steps to be better stewards of our time, we have to have a realistic idea of how we are using it now. To that end, an exercise may be helpful. Keep a log of how you spend your waking hours during the next week. It would probably be best to tally up the figures at the same time each day — perhaps just before you go to sleep. Use the categories in the following chart unless you can think of some that would better suit your round of activities.

	S	M	T	W	T	F	S	TOTAL
MEALS Include food preparation, eating, clean-up	—	—	—	—	—	—	—	—
VOCATIONAL WORK Include hours spent at your principal task and travel time	—	—	—	—	—	—	—	—
CHORES Include time spent on home maintenance, cleaning, laundry, shopping, errands	—	—	—	—	—	—	—	—
LEISURE Include time spent on hobbies, watching television, etc.	—	—	—	—	—	—	—	—
PHYSICAL HEALTH Include all activities aimed at maintaining your physical well-being, including exercise, brushing teeth, showering, etc.	—	—	—	—	—	—	—	—
MENTAL HEALTH Include time spent reading and attending classes, lectures, discussion groups, etc.	—	—	—	—	—	—	—	—
SPIRITUAL HEALTH Include time spent in formal and informal worship, devotions, and prayer	—	—	—	—	—	—	—	—
SERVICE Include all time devoted specifically to others	—	—	—	—	—	—	—	—

At the end of the week, tally up the numbers and work out some rough percentages. Did you find any surprises? How much time do you devote to God and others relative to the amount of time you spend on yourself? If you find areas in which you could stand to be a better care-manager of your time, can you think of any specific trade-offs you would be willing to make?

QUESTIONS FOR DISCUSSION

1. Faced with limited medical resources, physicians in Great Britain recently denied heart surgery to a patient on the grounds that he smoked cigarettes and hence would be less likely to benefit from the procedure than others. What do you think of their stewardship decision in this case? Would you have made a similar judgment about the patient's stewardship of his life? Have you made any decisions in the care-managing of your own life that would put you at similar risk? If so, how serious do you consider them to be?

2. Most of us find at some point in our lives that God has entrusted us not only with responsibility for our own lives but also with responsibilities for the lives of others. Have you ever had to make a life-or-death decision for someone else — a child or an aged parent, for example? If so, what sorts of considerations influenced your decision? If not, how would you counsel someone who had to make such a decision?

3. Protests by animal rights activists regularly make it into the news these days. How valid do you feel their concerns are? Should animals be sacrificed for medical research? For cosmetics testing? For other product safety testing? That is to say, how far do you think God's call for us to care for life extends?

4. In a recent survey of people who reported that they didn't exercise because they didn't have enough time to do so, it was found that on average the respondents watched over three hours of television a day. We all tend to find time for the things that are most important to us. What aspects of your life have the highest priority? Do you feel your activities accurately reflect these priorities? If not, can you think of any specific ways to change the balance?

5. The Bible places a very strong emphasis on the observance of the Sabbath as a natural interruption in the world of daily labor. The creation story suggests that God means this rhythm of work and rest to be a fundamental part of the created order. Do you experience genuine rest on the Sabbath? Are you restored and vitalized each week, or do the stresses of habits of the workweek encroach on your day of worship? What are some of the things you think God wants you to experience on the Sabbath? Can you think of any ways in which you could more fully turn this time over to such experiences?

8. Gifts of the Holy Spirit

You will receive power when the Holy Spirit has come upon you; and you will be my witnesses.

ACTS 1:8

God's Gift of the Spirit

We get and give gifts on any number of occasions in our culture. Some are perfunctory, some obligatory. But few things touch us and stay with us like gifts given in love — a flower from a child, a ring from a suitor, an offer to baby-sit from a close friend. We know that God gives all gifts in love, but we are so utterly surrounded with them every day that it is easy to take them for granted. In this chapter, we will look at a special category of these gifts: the gifts of the Holy Spirit.

The Bible clearly teaches that the Holy Spirit gives gifts to Christians. "Now there are varieties of gifts, but the same Spirit. . . . To each is given the manifestation of the Spirit for the common good" (1 Cor. 12:4, 7). For a long time, the subject of the gifts of the Spirit was not much discussed in Christian circles, but more recently there has been a resurgence in interest in the biblical teachings about spiritual gifts. Even so, relatively few Christians understand their spiritual gifts or how to make proper use of them.

Consider Sarah, a woman in my church who became a Christian in her early teens. She was extremely shy, and although she participated in her Sunday school class with interest and was active in the congregation's youth group, she backed away from anything that looked like a leadership role. In fact, more than once she said she would stop coming if she were forced into an up-front role. But we noticed that Sarah had a great interest in learning and that she was far more open to sharing in smaller groups. This evident interest, along with other indications, led a number of our congregation's leaders to suspect that a spiritual gift of teaching lay hidden beneath her shyness.

After a good deal of persuasion, Sarah finally agreed to become part of a three-member teaching team, on the condition that she would play only a supportive role and the other two people would be the "main teachers." They taught a children's class, which Sarah considered to be the least threatening. She attended some teaching training classes and gradually began to extend her leadership activity with the children. Her gift grew. She fell in love with the children and began sharing her love with them in ways she had never thought possible. Soon it was a teaching team of two persons, and then there was one — Sarah. She became a wonderfully gifted teacher and has shared her Jesus with countless numbers of children in the years since.

Because Sarah gave so much of herself, going far beyond the duties of ordinary teaching and sharing, we who watched her grow were inclined to think that she had a gift of the Spirit, rather than a simple talent, for teaching. We will take up the distinction between spiritual gifts and talents later in this chapter; at this point, I would simply note the following characteristics of spiritual gifts:

- they come to us from God through the Holy Spirit;
- they are given, not earned, as an expression of God's grace;
- they are meant to be employed for God's purposes, not personal glory or profit of any sort;
- they are given to all Christians, not just clergy;
- they are given to promote and enable Christian ministry and service;
- they are meant to strengthen the church, the Body of Christ;
- they should not be coveted or envied;
- they have to be properly care-managed by Christian stewards.

Some of the more important descriptions of the gifts of the Holy Spirit appear in Romans 12:6-8; 1 Corinthians 12:4-11, 28; and Ephesians 4:11. Stop and read these passages in the light of the characteristics listed above.

The Source of Spiritual Gifts

The Bible exhibits many approaches to the concept of spiritual gifts, but perhaps the key approach is to consider the source of the gifts and the reasons for their being given.

The Body of Christ, the living church, is God's ultimate goal. God is building the living church. God's grace is the source of all gifts of the Holy Spirit. The Greek term for "grace" is *charis,* and the closely related term *charisma* means "gift" or "gift of grace." Paul wrote, "Each of us was given grace according to the measure of Christ's gift. Therefore it is said, 'When he ascended on high . . . he gave gifts to his people'" (Eph. 4:7-8). In God's own way and time, the Holy Spirit imparts gifts to Christians to equip them for discipleship. You and I enter into partnership with God as we make use of these gifts. The Bible says that we are workers together with God: "For we are God's servants [stewards], working together; you are God's field, God's building" (1 Cor. 3:9). God is the source of the gifts, and we are the recipients of the gifts by which the church is being built.

Today the term *charisma* has come to mean a special, somewhat elusive quality that makes people attractive to others. But it is important to note that in the biblical perspective, charisma centers not in special individuals but in the grace of God from which the gifts of the Holy Spirit originate. The whole church is charismatic as it participates in the gifts and graces of God.

In approaching the subject of spiritual gifts, we need to think of the purpose for which they have been given rather than peculiar phenomena in their own right. For example, if we focus on the comparatively spectacular gift of speaking in tongues apart from the larger context of the purpose of spiritual gifts, we can easily become mired in pointless speculation and controversy. Spiritual gifts are entrusted to all believers, and we are called to care-manage them as we do all things that God entrusts to us.

The Purpose of Spiritual Gifts

When Paul listed some of the spiritual gifts in his letter to the Ephesians, he added that their purpose is "to equip the saints for the work of ministry, for building up the body of Christ, until all of us come to the unity of the faith and of the knowledge of the Son of God, to maturity, to the measure of the full stature of Christ" (4:12-13). Each Christian has a task to perform in building up the church; God gives us spiritual gifts to equip us for this work.

It is God's will that each Christian use her or his spiritual gifts. Note the biblical emphasis on this point:

To each is given the manifestation of the Spirit for the common good. (1 Cor. 12:7)

All these are activated by one and the same Spirit, who allots to each one individually just as the Spirit chooses. (1 Cor. 12:11)

As new Christians become stewards through their new relationship with God in Christ, they receive spiritual gifts as an emblem of this new relationship. Paul suggests both unity and variety in the same breath: "Now there are varieties of gifts, but the same Spirit; and there are varieties of services, but the same Lord; and there are varieties of activities, but it is the same God who activates all of them in everyone" (1 Cor. 12:4-6). In his book *Gifts of the Spirit*, Kenneth Cain Kinghorn states, "All spiritual gifts have their source in God — here is unity. God distributes a plurality of spiritual gifts among the Christian community — here is variety" (p. 27).

Biblical Listings of Gifts

Spiritual gifts are mentioned throughout Scripture. Different scholars have drawn up different lists of spiritual gifts based on different readings of which passages of Scripture contain lists of gifts. It would not be particularly profitable for us to go into the subtleties of their arguments here; it will be enough for us to get a sense of the broad outlines of the topic by looking at the four principal and undisputed lists, noting their similarities and differences.

Romans 12:6-8	prophecy, ministry, teaching, exhorting, giving, leading, compassion
1 Corinthians 12:4-11	wisdom, knowledge, faith, healing, miracles, prophecy, discernment of spirits, speaking in tongues, interpretation of tongues
1 Corinthians 12:28	apostleship, prophecy, teaching, miracles, healing, helping, leadership, speaking in tongues
Ephesians 4:11	apostleship, prophecy, evangelism, pastoral skills, teaching

Prophecy is mentioned in all four passages, teaching in three, and the remainder only once or twice. There is no clear logic to the various scriptural listings, no systematic ordering from passage to passage. Indeed, it is quite possible that the lists are not meant to be exhaustive. Perhaps you could name additional spiritual gifts. To cite one modest example, I have sometimes wondered if there is a gift of ushering. In my travels to many churches, once in a while I am cared for by an usher who truly seems to be gifted for that task, compared to others who simply do a job. There is no question that those who use their gifts build the living Body of Christ.

The gift of prophecy, which appears in all four lists, is not some kind of fortune telling. The term as it is used in these contexts refers to sharing with others new inspiration and illumination under the leadership of the Holy Spirit. This is something every church needs on a regular basis. Many churches today expect this to be provided by the pastor. However, we should recognize that laypeople may be equally gifted to bring new ideas, inspiration, and illumination to a congregation in board and committee meetings, Sunday school classes, small group gatherings, and the like.

What the Spiritual Gifts Are Not

There remains a fair amount of confusion about the nature of spiritual gifts in Christian circles. The gifts are often confused with associated biblical concepts. Before we proceed, then, perhaps it would be helpful to reflect on what spiritual gifts are *not*.

They Are Not "the Gift of the Holy Spirit"

The Bible clearly distinguishes between the "gift of the Holy Spirit" (singular) and the "gifts of the Holy Spirit" (plural). In Peter's first recorded sermon to a large crowd, he answered their question "What should we do?" by saying, "Repent, and be baptized every one of you in the name of Jesus Christ so that your sins may be forgiven; and you will receive the gift of the Holy Spirit" (Acts 2:38). In other passages, we read that Christians are baptized in the Spirit (Acts 11:15-16), marked by the seal of the Spirit (Eph. 1:13), and born of the Spirit (John 3:6). These and other accounts tell us that the presence of God's Spirit is at the heart of the new life of a Christian. But the gift of the Spirit — the process by which God comes to dwell within us — is different from the gifts of the Spirit that God offers us through the agency of the indwelling Spirit.

Paul addressed the church at Corinth with a rather pointed question: "Do you not know that you are God's temple, and that God's Spirit dwells in you?" (1 Cor. 3:16). To what degree do you sense the presence of the indwelling Spirit of God as a reality in your Christian journey? Can you think of some times when you were distinctly aware of the Spirit's presence? Is there a common thread in these occasions? What place does the Holy Spirit have in the life of your congregation? Can you think of one or more individuals in your congregation whose lives seem clearly marked by the presence of the Spirit? What signs of it do you see?

They Are Not the "Fruit of the Spirit"

Galatians 5:16-26 distinguishes between "works of the flesh" (e.g., impurity, idolatry, anger, envy) and "the fruit of the Spirit," which is "love, joy, peace, patience, kindness, generosity, faithfulness, gentleness, and self-control." All those in whom the Spirit dwells should be guided by the Spirit to bear this fruit.

The fruit of the Spirit is different from the gifts of the Spirit in two ways. First, the gifts are special empowerments to action, whereas the fruit are expressions of action. For example, Romans 12:8 refers to the gift of giving, and this gift can be expressed in the fruit of generosity; similarly, the gift of compassion can be expressed in the fruit of gentleness. Second, Christians receive different gifts — you may have the gift of wisdom, your neighbor the gift of evangelism, your pastor the gift of ministry, and so on — but all Christians are expected to manifest the fruits of the Spirit. We will return to this point later.

As you walk your journey with Christ, which of the fruits of the Spirit are usually evident in your life? Which fruits are less evident? What can you do to nurture them?

They Are Not Merely Special Abilities

Most of us can point to a handful of special abilities in ourselves and others. Everybody seems to have a special knack for something. Some people seem to be born with the gift to make music or to deal with numbers or to catch rainbow trout or to rebuild carburetors. All these natural talents are gifts from

God and hence worthy of diligent stewardship. However, the gifts in this category do not appear in any of the listings of spiritual gifts in the New Testament. On the other hand, as I suggested earlier, it is by no means certain that the biblical listings are exhaustive. Perhaps we could consider natural talents to be spiritual gifts to the extent that they are used to extend the life, growth, and ministry of the church.

They Are Not Spiritual Disciplines

Spiritual disciplines are intentional activities such as prayer, fasting, Bible study, service, giving, and contemplative reflection. We engage in such activities to make our lives as Christians more effective, vital, meaningful, happy, fruitful, and joyful. When we first accept Jesus Christ into our lives, we are spiritually immature. Spiritual disciplines provide structure for the growth to which we are called. They are distinct from gifts of the Spirit in that they focus on personal edification rather than the edification of the church.

Spiritual Gifts Close to Home

Having established some criteria for discerning spiritual gifts, let's try to identify those that are in use in your congregation and your personal life. Begin with yourself. List any spiritual gifts you have and try to be specific about how you are using them.

_____

_____

_____

_____

_____

_____

_____

_____

_____

Now join forces with others and conduct an inventory of your congregation's spirituals gifts. Link the names of specific individuals with gifts you have observed in them and note what use they have made of the gifts.

Name   **Gift and Application**

_____   _____

                       _____

_____   _____

                       _____

_____   _____

                       _____

_____   _____

                       _____

Looking over both these lists, do you see any patterns? Are any sorts of gifts missing or inadequately developed? Are you aware of any gifts in yourself or others that are just emerging and that may need to be refined or developed further? What can you and your congregation do to encourage and nurture these gifts? If some gifts are missing altogether, should you look outside your congregation to find people who could supply them? Can you think of any other remedies?

It is important to be aware of the gifts that the Holy Spirit gives us. It can be so easy to neglect such gifts or even to avoid looking for them in the first place, because we know that every gift we receive from God comes with an expectation that we will do something with it. But if we can overcome our reluctance, we will be rewarded — and not only us but the whole body of Christ. If you feel uncertain or inadequate to discern what gift or gifts you feel you may have, talk with those who know you best in the context of your church ministry and involvement. Talk to your pastor. Listen to what others tell you about their perceptions of your spiritual gifts and, with their help and God's help, make an effort to develop them for the glory of God and the edification of the church.

QUESTIONS FOR DISCUSSION

1. The spiritual gift of speaking in tongues is mentioned twice in the biblical lists we surveyed, and the gift of interpreting tongues is mentioned once. These gifts are a point of controversy in the church today. What is the official position of your church regarding these gifts? Do you agree with that position? Why?

2. The list of spiritual gifts in 1 Corinthians 12:28 includes the gifts of healing and working miracles. Do you believe that miracles still take place in today's church? Do you know any Christian who exercises the gift of working miracles today? Have you or anyone you know ever sought miraculous healing for yourself or a loved one through the agency of a Christian who professed to have this spiritual gift? If so, what was the result? If not, why not?

3. What does your congregation do to encourage the discernment, development, and validation of spiritual gifts today? Are you satisfied with the efforts being made in this regard? If so, name some specific ways in which these efforts have served you and others you know well. If not, suggest some ways in which you believe your church could do a better job in this area.

4. What do you feel is the most important spiritual gift in your life at the moment? How are you using it? Is there any gift you wish you had? Any gift you are just as thankful you don't have? Why?

5. Do you know anyone that you feel is not making use of a spiritual gift? Do you think it falls within the range of appropriate stewardship to confront such a person with your feelings on this issue? Have you ever done so? If so, what was the result? If not, why not? How would you react if someone confronted you with a suggestion that you are not nurturing a spiritual gift of your own?

9. God's Gifts of Relationships

The LORD is my shepherd. . . . Even though I walk through the darkest valley, I fear no evil; for you are with me.

PSALM 23:1, 4

For the past twenty-nine years I've been enjoying a relationship with a Bartlett pear tree. It was already quite old when I became its care-manager, but now it is ancient. There are holes in some of its main branches, and one whole side of the tree broke off years ago, leaving it with an odd shape. Six years ago I planted another pear tree nearby because it looked as though the old tree was beyond hope. But it doesn't die.

I feed it, prune it, care for it, and every August I pick a bountiful crop. When other fruit trees are having off years, this tree goes right on producing an unbelievable amount of delicious pears. Sometimes I just lean against it and marvel at its stamina, its productiveness, and its beauty. I don't want it to die. That pear tree and I have a beautiful relationship, at least from my perspective!

Most people have many relationships during a lifetime — relationships with the God of the universe, with friends, family, neighbors, coworkers, birds and animals, trees. We even develop what might be called relationships with inanimate things — a comfortable pair of shoes, a dependable car, an old covered bridge where we have spent many an hour day-dreaming. As a nation, we have a variety of shifting relationships with other nations and peoples. As a species, we have a vital relationship with the fragile world in which we live.

Some of our relationships are neutral, generating neither positive nor negative feelings, but in most cases we have a significant emotional investment in them. Some we cherish, nurture, and protect. Others cause us endless pain, irritation, and stress. All of them are close to the heart of what makes us the people we are. Let's take a closer look at their significance by examining two basic categories of relationships — "vertical" and "horizontal."

Vertical Relationships

I have chosen to use the traditional terms *vertical* and *horizontal* to refer to relationships with God and other persons, respectively, even though I realize there are certain problems with the metaphors. In using the term *vertical* to refer to spiritual relationships, I do not mean to suggest that God is distant from us, residing solely in the heavens above. God is very much with us in our day-to-day activities, sustaining the whole of the created order moment by moment, breathing life into the church, dwelling in our hearts when offered the invitation to do so. We encounter God in three persons and relate uniquely to each — to God as Creator/Owner, to Jesus Christ as Savior and Lord, to the Holy Spirit as Sanctifier and Comforter. Each relationship is equally essential to our Christian lives, and we impoverish ourselves spiritually if we emphasize or value any one of them disproportionately. We do well to ask ourselves how we relate to God, to Jesus Christ, and to the Holy Spirit, but perhaps the more important question is how God relates to us.

God's Relationship with Humankind

The history of vertical relationships is as old as the history of the human race. In fact, the Bible indicates that Adam's relationship with God preceded his relationship with Eve. In this long history, one of the first relationships to emerge was that of stewardship on God's behalf. In Genesis 1:28-30 we read that God turned over the whole of the created order to human beings for care-managing.

Almost from the outset, we violated our relationship with God and shrunk in shame from that violation. Genesis 3:8 offers us a tantalizing glimpse of what the relationship must have been like before the disruption: God came to the garden at the time of the evening breeze. I like to think that God was arriving for a caring visit, an evening of sharing. But when God called his creatures, they were off hiding, fearful and ashamed. They had broken the beautiful relationship. Life on earth has not been the same since that evening visit.

Even so, God never gives up! Our covenanting God keeps wanting and trying to have a meaningful relationship with any who will respond. In Genesis 8:20-22, we read that after the flood Noah offered burnt offerings on an altar. At that time, God promised "I will never again curse the ground because of humankind." Later God covenanted with Abram: "I will make you a great nation, and I will bless you" (Gen. 12:2). There are records of many similar covenants in the Old Testament.

The New Testament indicates that all the sacrifices prescribed in the Old Testament were realized and surpassed by Christ's sacrifice on the cross. Jesus' love for a sinful, undeserving humanity replaced all altars (Heb. 9). Love is the key word, just as much today as it was in the establishment of the early church. God's love reaches out to us through Jesus Christ (John 17:22-26).

We are called to respond to God's love with all of our being — with all our heart, soul, mind, and strength (Mark 12:30). Can we open our minds to God so totally that our very patterns of thought and action enable us to enjoy being children of God? In what ways can we enjoy God's thoughts? Can we pursue reflections on life that include God-centeredness in our daily walk? Is God real, vital, and present in each of our daily agendas?

Pause for a moment and think about your relationship with God. Then turn your attention to the following:

1. To the extent that you know biblical history, give some illustrations of events or occasions when God moved in the direction of human beings while providing care, guidance, direction, strength, and the like.

_____

_____

_____

_____

_____

_____

_____

_____

2. Give some biblical illustrations of times when Jesus moved toward people and provided love and compassion.

_____

_____

_____

_____

_____

_____

_____

_____

3. Give some biblical illustrations of times when the Holy Spirit was active in the lives of people.

_____

_____

_____

_____

_____

_____

_____

4. Give examples of instances in which God has touched, moved, or blessed people you know — friends, family, church members, coworkers, or others.

_____

_____

_____

_____

_____

_____

5. Think of your own faith journey and list some occasions on which God has been specially close to you. Indicate what it was that convinced you of God's presence.

_____

_____

_____

_____

_____

_____

Your Relationship with God

Meaningful relationships build from trust. Do you trust God? In what way? Can God trust you?

Much of life is uncertain. We cannot know for certain what turns may await us. We can look forward to certain joys and happinesses, but we will also have to face some hurts and disappointments. How does it affect your feelings for God when you are hurt, when you are disappointed, when you are let down by family, the church, or friends? When the valley is deepest, can you still trust God?

Now reverse your perspective: How do you think God would describe your relationship? Take a few minutes to be quiet and seek to discern God's thoughts in prayer. Write down the words or phrases you think God might use to describe your relationship:

_____

_____

_____

_____

_____

_____

_____

Using one or two words, describe your present awareness/relation with each aspect of the Trinity:

with God the Parent (Creator/Owner)

_____

_____

_____

_____

_____

_____

_____

_____

with Jesus Christ (Savior and Lord)

_____

_____

_____

_____

_____

_____

with the Holy Spirit (Sanctifier and Comforter)

_____

_____

_____

_____

_____

_____

Many people find it difficult to describe their relationship with the triune God. We claim a relationship with God but rarely take time to identify or clarify it. But some degree of understanding is vital if we are to make good our promise to be faithful stewards of this relationship. God eagerly awaits each contact we make. The opportunity to develop a significant faith relationship with God rests with us.

Psalm 23 is perhaps the most familiar passage of the Bible among both churched and unchurched people. One reason for its popularity is its profession of confidence in God. Clearly and unequivocally, the author gives reason after reason for his trust in God. Who can argue with his proclamation that "even though I walk through the darkest valley, I fear no evil; for you are with me" (v. 4)?

Try writing your own Psalm. Think about reasons why you trust God. Write statements that express your confidence in God. Make it your own by using the sorts of words and phrases you use every day. Make it your offering to God today!

_____

_____

_____

_____

_____

_____

_____

_____

_____

_____

_____

_____

_____

Strengthening Your Relationship with God

Jan and Myron Chartier have written about God's love for us in a book entitled *Nurturing Faith in the Family.* "From our study of the life and teachings of Jesus within the context of the whole Bible," they say, "we have identified seven mutually interdependent dimensions of God's love for humanity. . . . Caring; Responsive; Accountable; Giving; Knowing; Respectful; Forgiving" (p. 41). These words summarize the ingredients of God's love for us and suggest how we can respond in a similar fashion.

No relationship with God is ever complete or final, especially in this life. There is always room for our relationships with God to grow and deepen. This is where the call to stewardship comes in: we have only twenty-four hours each day, and we must choose how to spend that time. What value do we place on taking time to develop a strong, meaningful relationship with each person of the triune God? Reading the Bible takes time. Going to Bible study groups takes time. Praying, worshiping, meditating, practicing our faith, and serving God and others takes time. How do we prioritize the daily experiences that take us into the presence of God? This is a stewardship issue.

God is always reaching out and seeking us, making the effort to be available to each of us, and yearning to improve our faith relationship. We often think of prayer as reaching out to God. We sometimes forget that God is constantly reaching out to us, that when we seek to pray, God is the initiator, and we are responding.

How can your relationship with God be enhanced? What can you do to strengthen your faith and trust in God. Which of the Chartiers' words do you need to work on to improve your relationship with God? Think about it, and make a list:

_____

_____

_____

_____

_____

_____

_____

_____

Horizontal Relationships

There is a potential for relationships in all our contacts with other people. We can even establish relationships with animals and the rest of our physical environment. Yet in the face of all this potential, most of us tend to establish relatively few long-lasting, significant relationships. One of the main reasons for this is that time is simply too short. But it is also the case that many of us are reluctant to invest the considerable amount of energy and trust that are necessary to sustain a significant relationship even if we know from experience that the rewards for doing so are great. Robert Fulghum refers to the benefits and costs of an extraordinary relationship in his best-selling little book *All I Really Need to Know I Learned in Kindergarten:*

> Remember Charles Boyer? Suave, dapper, handsome, graceful. Lover of the most famous and beautiful ladies of the silver screen. That was on camera and in the fan magazines. In real life it was different.
>
> There was only one woman. For forty-four years. His wife, Patricia. Friends said it was a lifelong love affair. They were no less lovers and friends and companions after forty-four years than after the first year.
>
> Then Patricia developed cancer of the liver. And though the doctors told Charles, he could not bear to tell her. And so he sat by her bedside to comfort and cheer. Day and night for six months. He could not change the inevitable. Nobody could. And Patricia died in his arms. Two days later Charles Boyer was also dead. By his own hand. He said he did not want to live without her. He said, "Her love was life to me."
>
> This was no movie. As I said, it's the real story — Charles Boyer's story.
>
> It's not for me to pass judgment on how he handled his grief. But it is for me to say that I am touched and comforted in a strange way. Touched by the depth of love behind the apparent sham of Hollywood love life. Comforted to know that a man and woman can love each other that much that long. (Pp. 32-33)

Such a love relationship as the Boyers' is beautiful. In a world where human relationships are often short-lived and shallow, a loving relationship like this stands out. Each of us yearns for warm, affirming, trusting relationships with other persons, whether in marriage or otherwise.

However chilly life may sometimes seem, it does present each of us with many opportunities to establish significant relationships. And as stewards of God, we are uniquely challenged to grasp these opportunities. How can we make the most of them? How many meaningful relationships can we handle?

Respect and mutual concern are basic to establishing important, satisfying, and meaningful relationships. We can find no better model for establishing healthy relationships than God, who not only anchors our most meaningful relationship but also promises to help develop and sustain our relationships with others. In this connection, it might be worthwhile to reflect on the Chartiers' "love words." They are as significant with respect to human relationships as they are with respect to our feelings about God, Christ, and the Holy Spirit. Consider them again, this time in light of your human relationships:

Caring
Accountable
Responsive
Giving
Knowing
Respectful
Forgiving

Incorporating these attributes in all of our relationships will increase their quality and extend their life.

Make a list of people with whom you now have meaningful, affirming relationships. After each name, place one or more of the "love words" that you feel describe your relationship.

_____

_____

_____

_____

_____

_____

_____

Now make a list of people with whom you would *like* to develop such relationships. Beside each name, place a word that identifies the context of the relationship, such as family, friend, work, school, neighbor, church, etc.

_____

_____

_____

_____

_____

_____

_____

Now prioritize your list, selecting the person to whom you would like to reach out first. What steps do you need to take to develop a stronger relationship with this person? Perhaps the first step should be to seek out God in prayer. Spend a few moments in prayer about fostering new and/or stronger relationships with God, this person, and others in your life.

QUESTIONS FOR DISCUSSION

1. In what ways does your relationship with God differ from your relationships with others? What aspects of each type of relationship are absent in the other? To what extent do you bring the two kinds of relationships together — for example, by discussing your horizontal relationships with God in prayer and discussing your vertical relationship with other Christians?

2. Have you ever experienced a situation in which you felt that your relationship with God was conflicting in some way with your relationship with someone else? Have you felt that a friendship was threatening your relationship with God in some way? If so, what did you do about it? If not, how would you respond to someone who complained of such a conflict in your friendship?

3. How many strong, healthy, deep friendships do you have with persons outside your family? Has marriage or some other significant relationship changed the number of your friendships over time? Do you feel this is

appropriate? Do you feel called by God to develop additional meaningful horizontal relationships?

4. Have you ever felt the need to slight one relationship in order to devote more time to another? For example, have you ever left your spouse home alone to take in some sort of entertainment with a friend, elected to visit members of your congregation instead of joining your family in some activity, or told friends you couldn't join them because you had to attend a child's school or sporting event? What factors did you weigh in making your decision, and what sorts of criteria proved to be decisive? Can you find any biblical basis for your decision?

5. Does your congregation make any efforts to improve relationships among its members? If yes, what are they, and how effective do you think they are? If no, can you suggest any ways in which your church could be more helpful?

Summary

Your formal reading and study of this workbook on biblical stewardship is now completed, but opportunities for you to pursue new approaches to stewardship are just beginning. It is my prayer that you are ready to be a steward who is faithful to what God has entrusted to you, a careful care-manager of all that belongs to God, and a confident confronter on God's behalf.

Effective stewards are among God's finest leaders. Stewards are Good News people, God's ambassadors to a lonely, hurting, and sometimes destructive world. Stewards, because of our family relationship with God, are living proof of a caring, involved God. Saint Francis of Assisi is quoted as having said, "Preach the gospel at all times. If necessary, use words." That is what being one of God's stewards is about. Our lives should model the stewardship that is on display in the Bible from Genesis to Revelation. People should be able to see in our lives — our very beings — that what we are about is God's business.

Both Old and New Testament illustrations of stewards suggest that faithfulness is a key ingredient in fulfilling the steward's role (Rom. 14:12; 1 Cor. 4:2). The faithfulness of good stewards is measured not merely by the adequacy of the job they do but more importantly by their attitude and the degree to which they understand and appropriately respond to God's commands. Any steward will be inadequate who forgets who the Boss is.

The New Testament characterizes the steward as a coworker with God. Isn't that exciting? As you embark on some new experiences in your steward's journey, may the fact that you are a coworker with God be your primary motivation. I believe I can promise you that at the conclusion of your journey you will hear these blessed words from the Creator/Owner/Sustainer God: "Well done, good and trustworthy slave [steward]; you have been trustworthy in a few things, I will put you in charge of many things; enter into the joy of your master" (Matt. 25:21).